Shoji & Kumiko

85 Vintage Designs

Toolemera Press
History Preserved
www.toolemerapress.com

Shoji & Kumiko: 85 Vintage Designs

International Standard Book Number
ISBN : 9781087817187
(Trade Paperback)

Published by
Toolemera Press
Wilmington, North Carolina
USA 28401

Shoji: A Japanese screen or sliding door.

Kumiko: A decorative yet practical Japanese woodworking system consisting of lattice pieces held together through precision joinery lacking any nails or other metal supports.

Shoji & Kumiko: 85 Vintage Designs features an original c1930 Japanese architectural proposal book of designs from the collection of Gary Roberts, Publisher: Toolemera Press.

Toolemera Press
History Preserved
www.toolemerapress.com

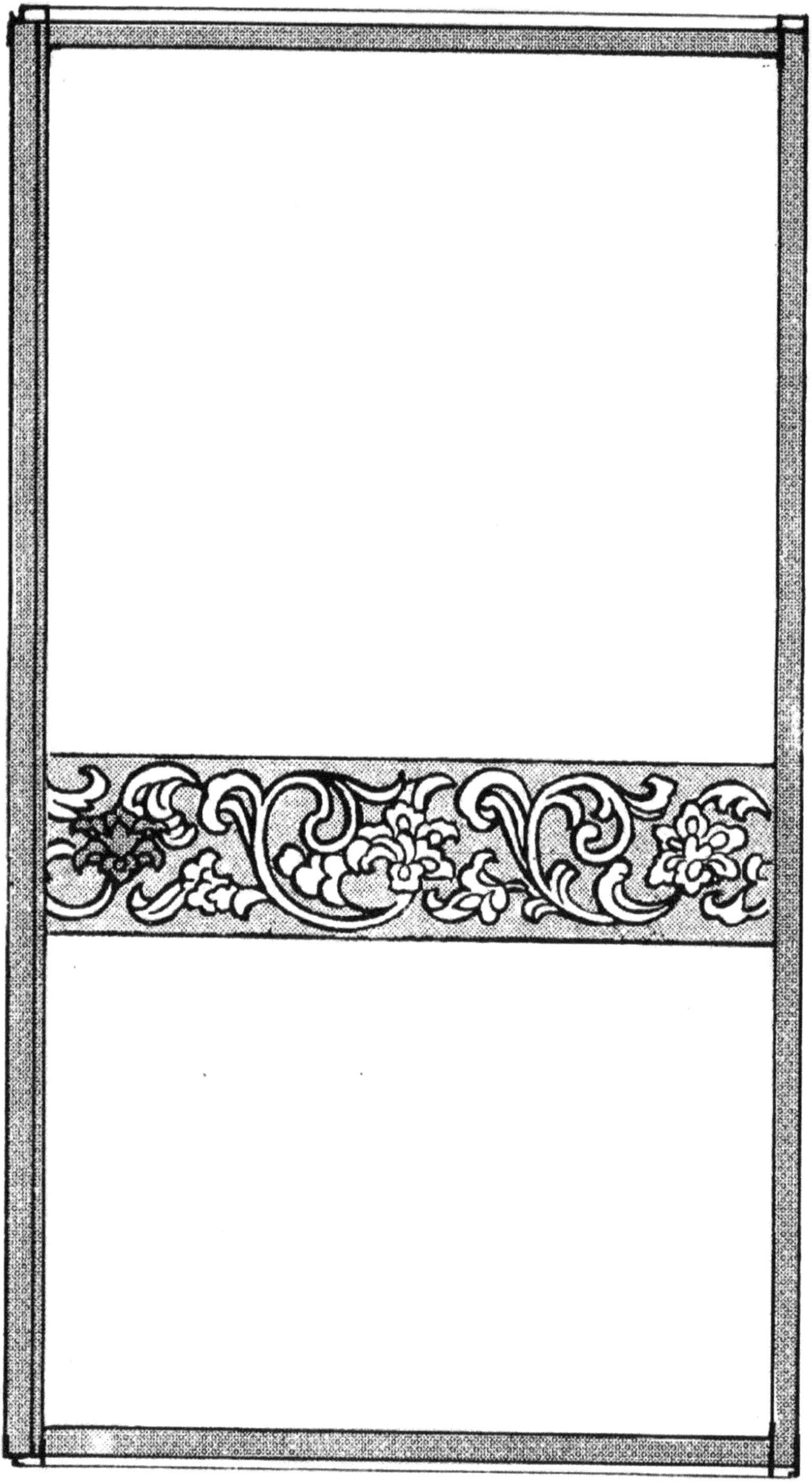

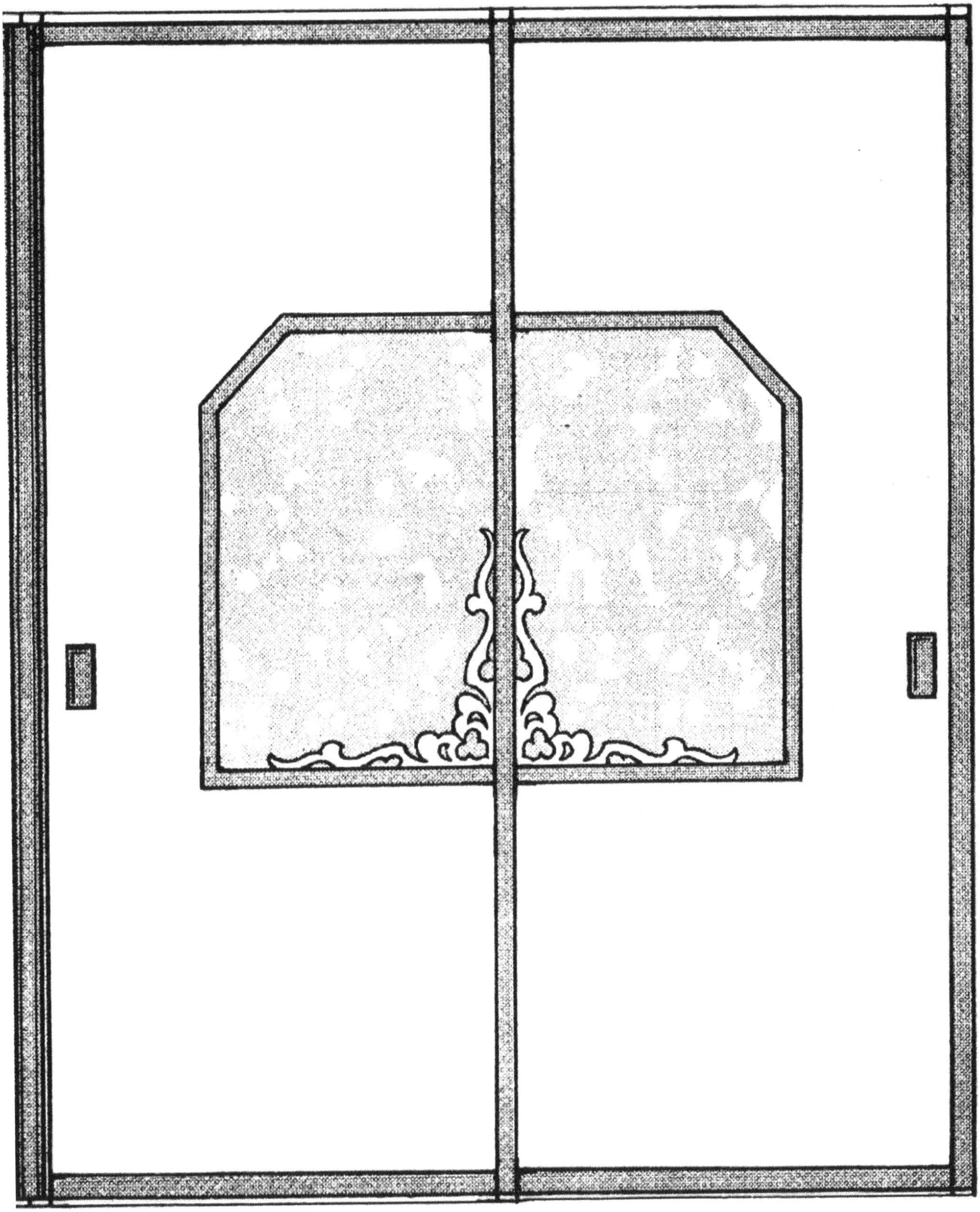

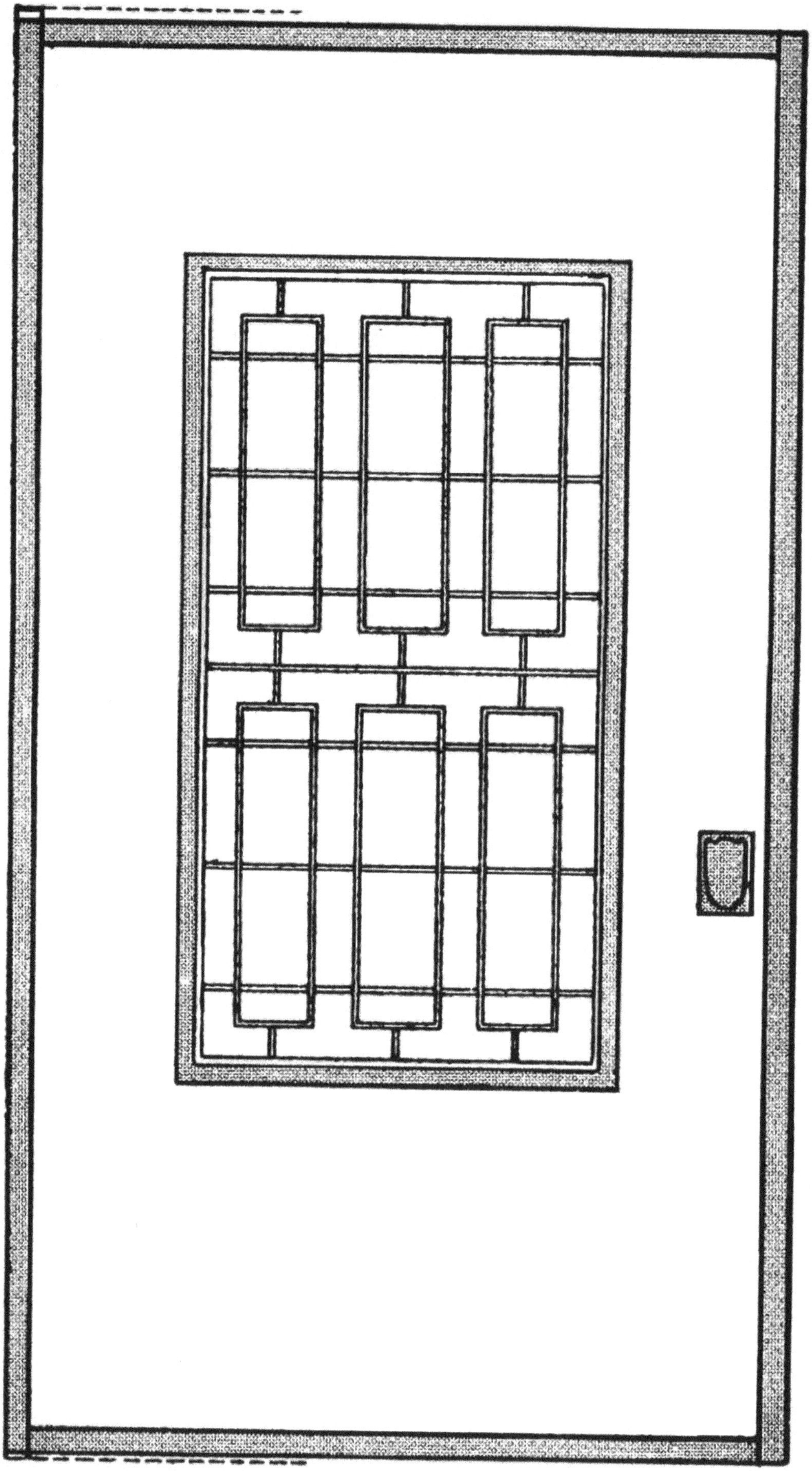

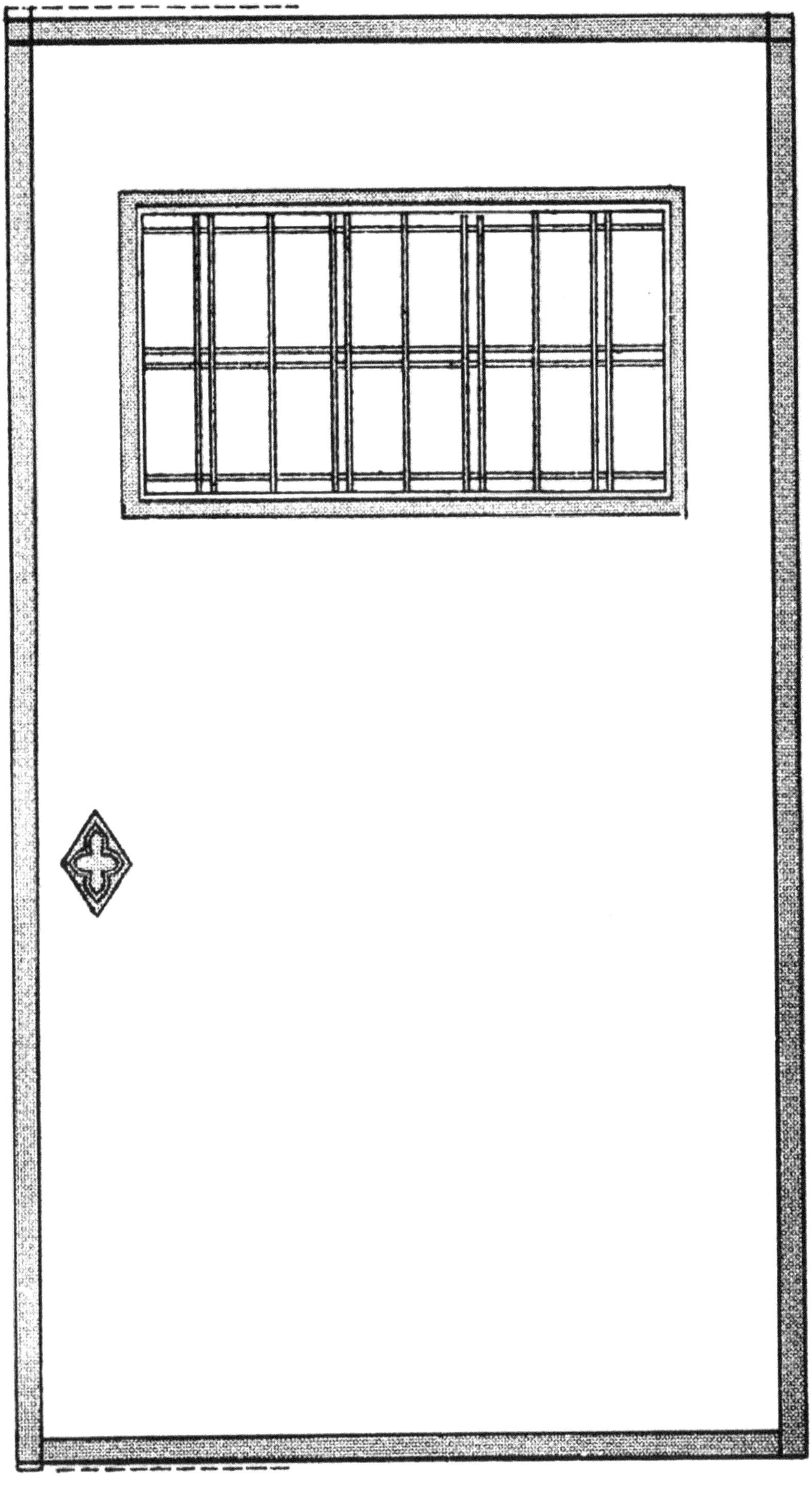

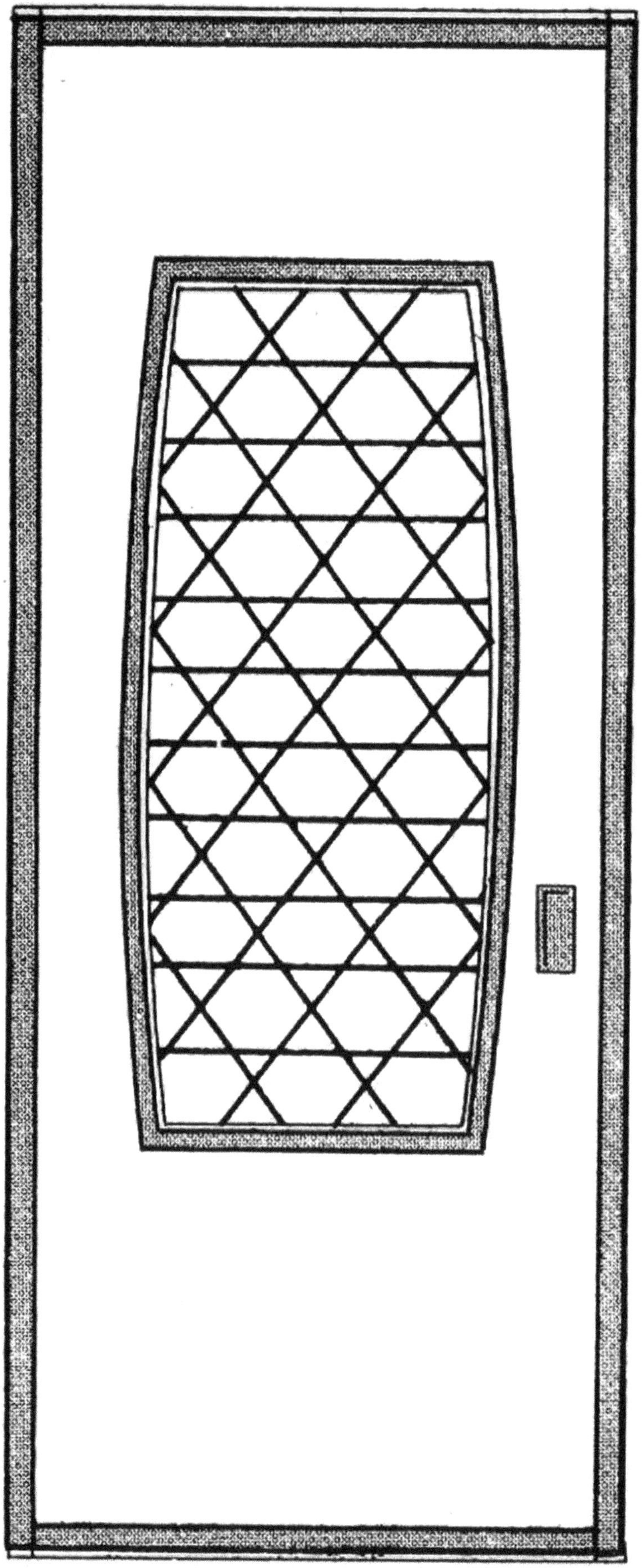

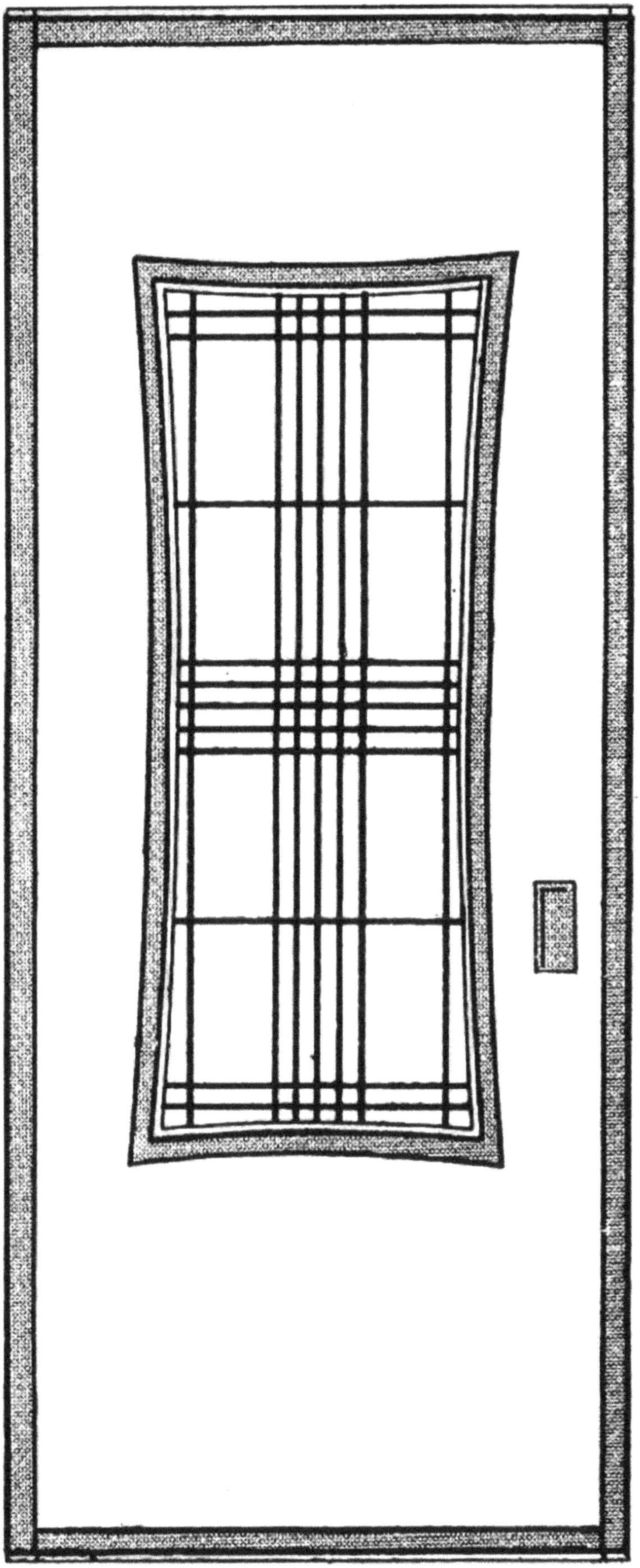

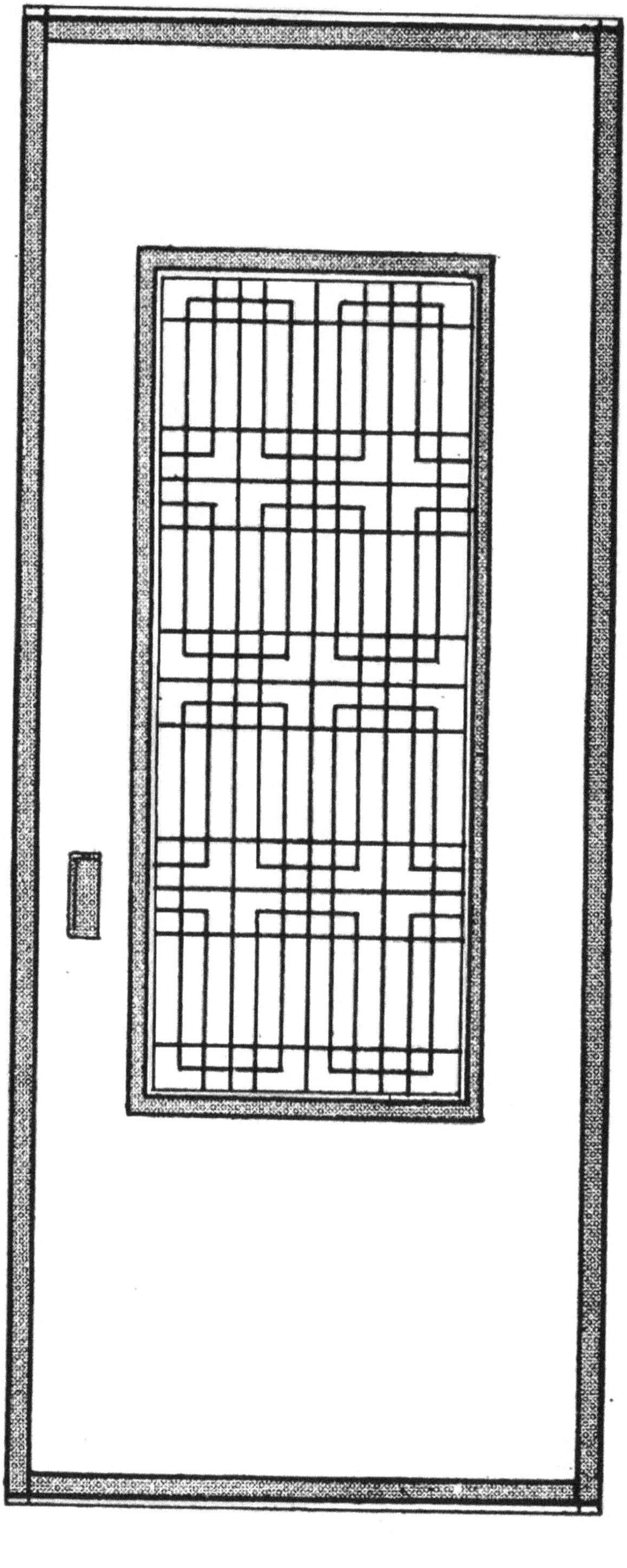

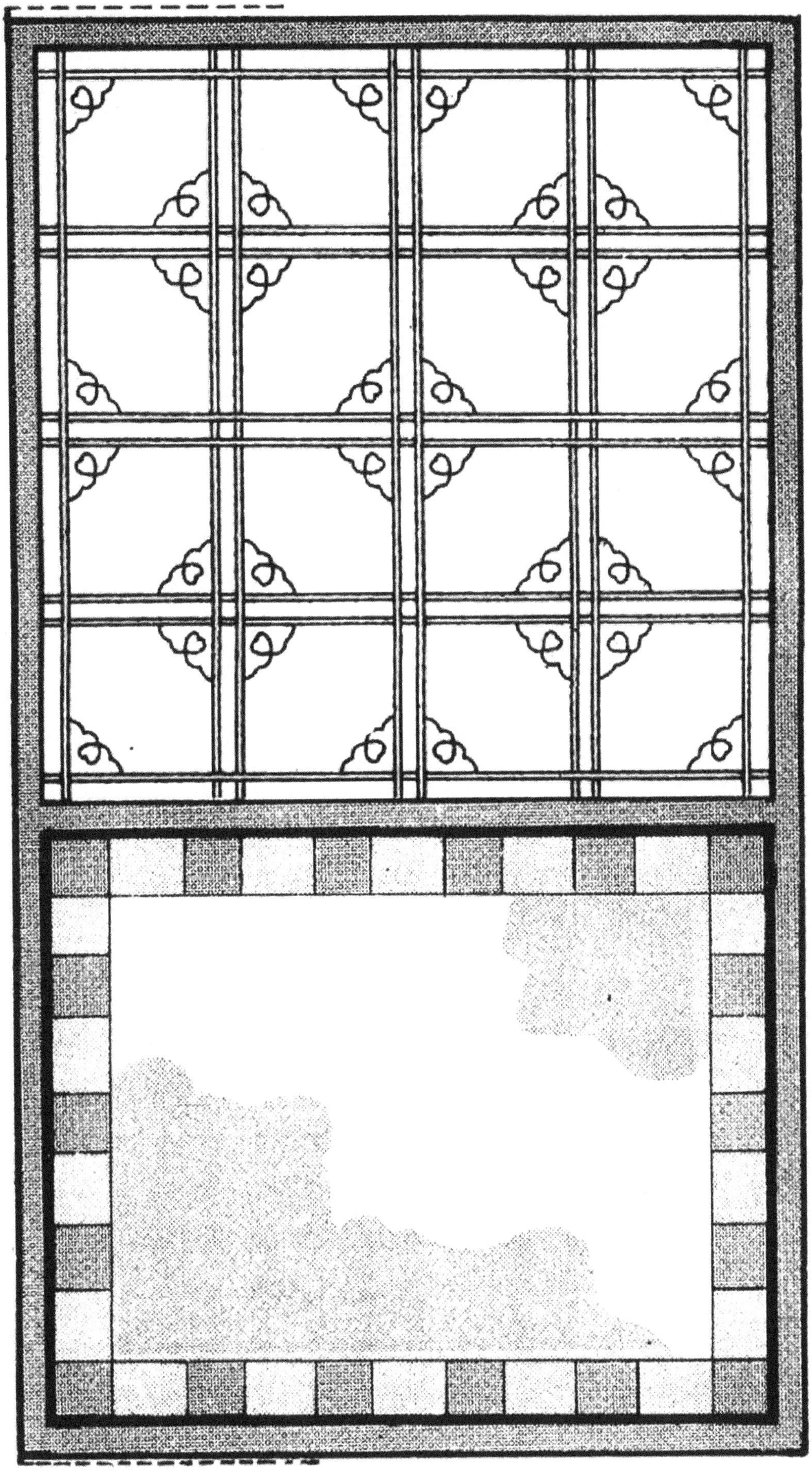

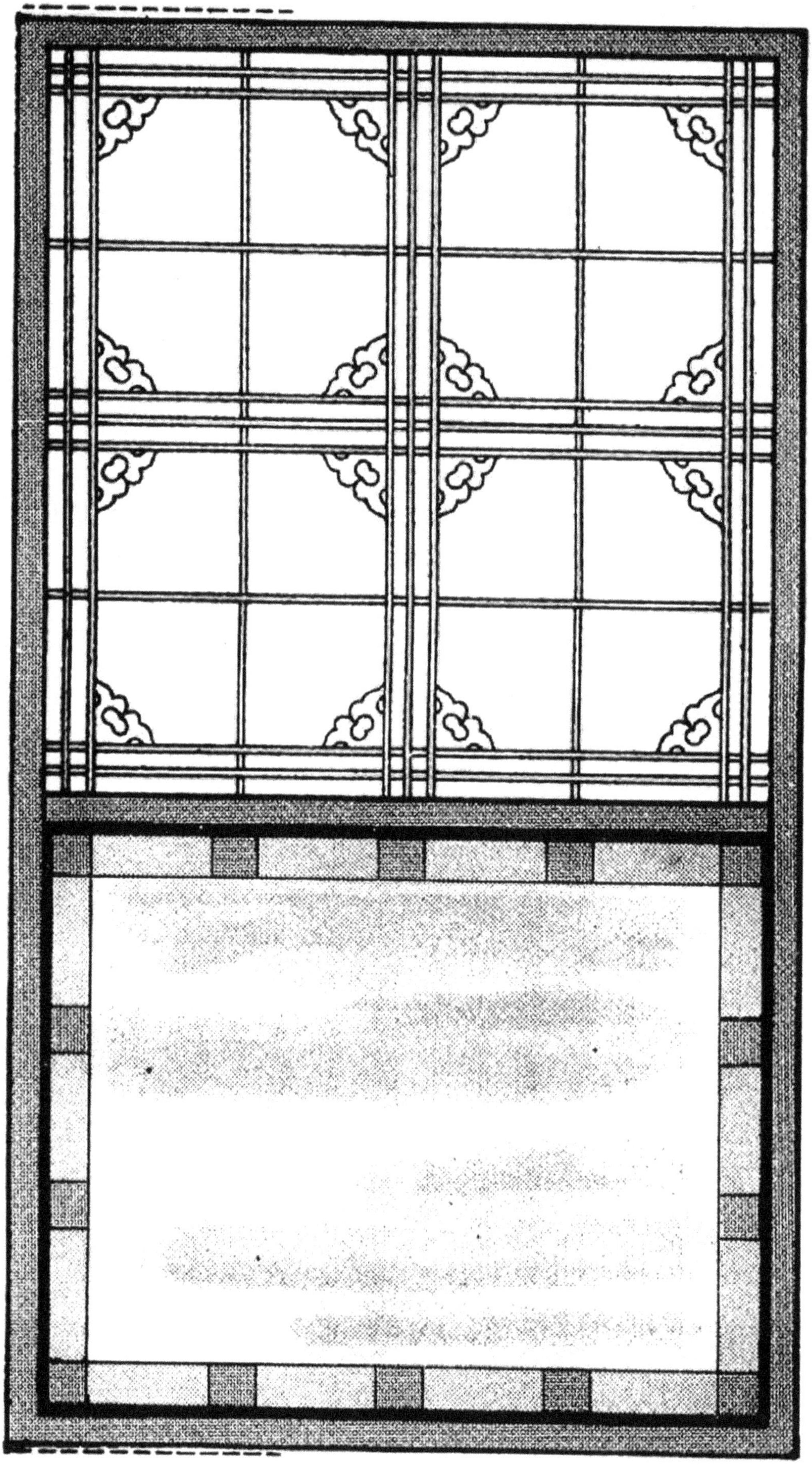

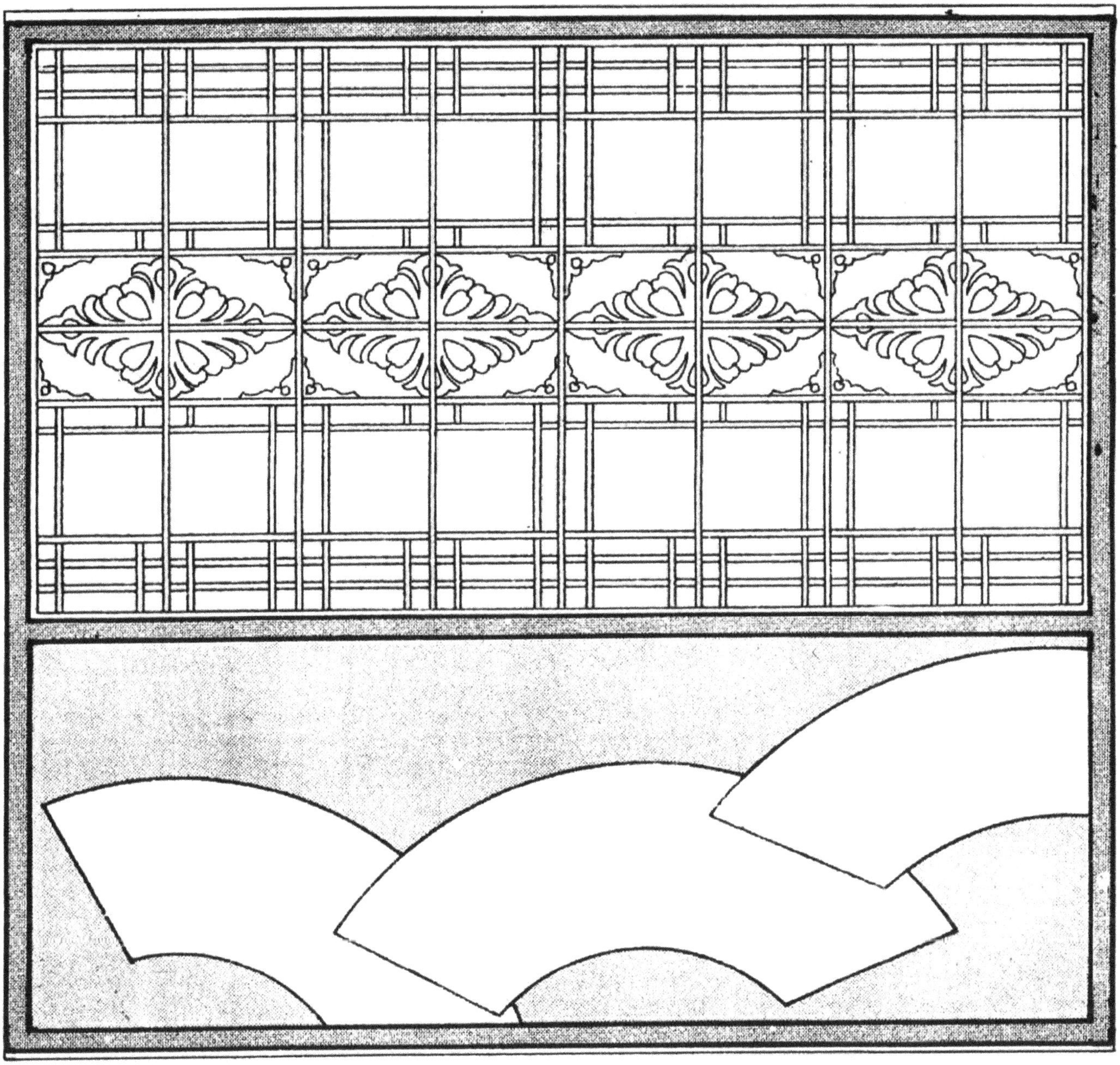

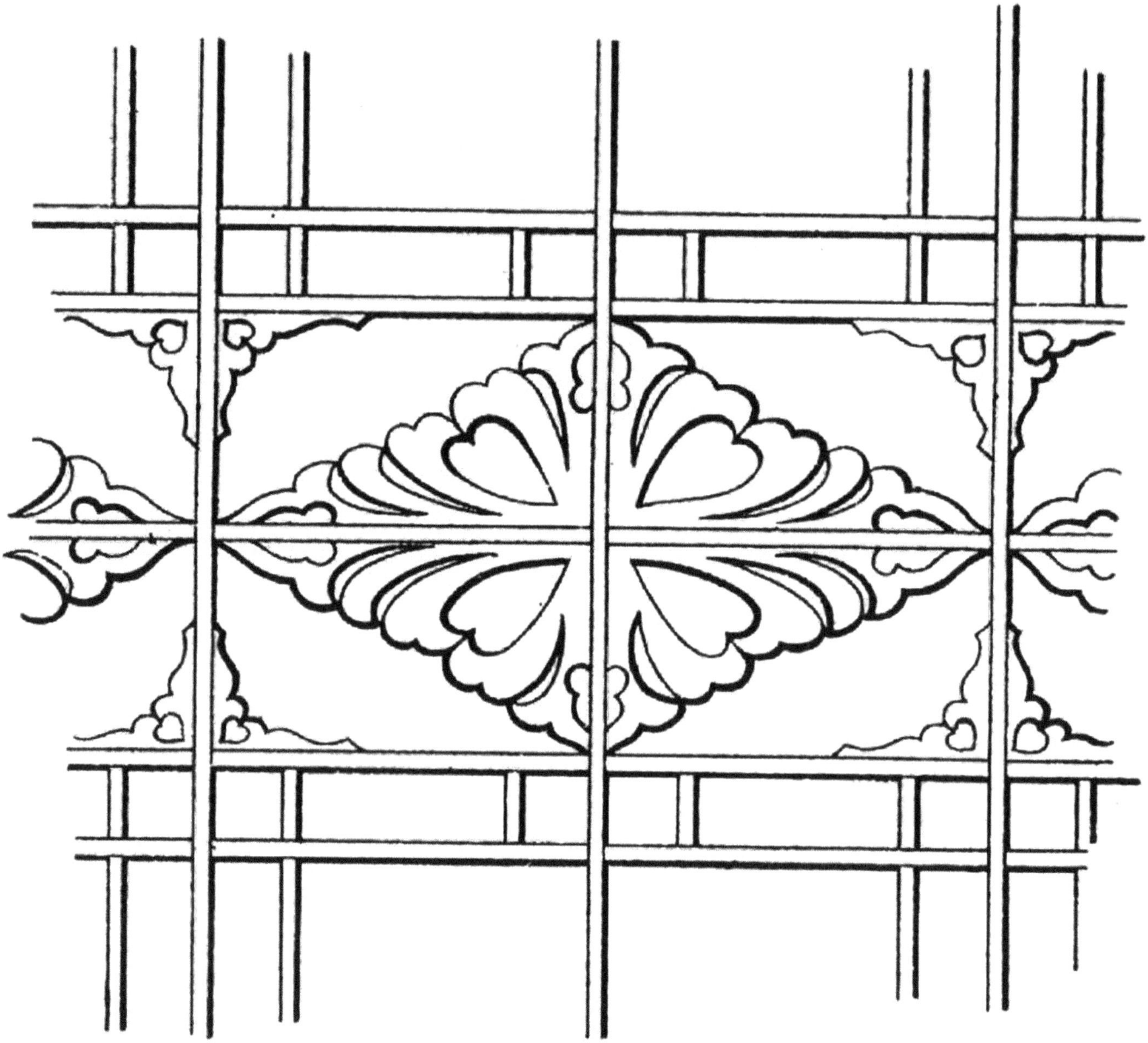

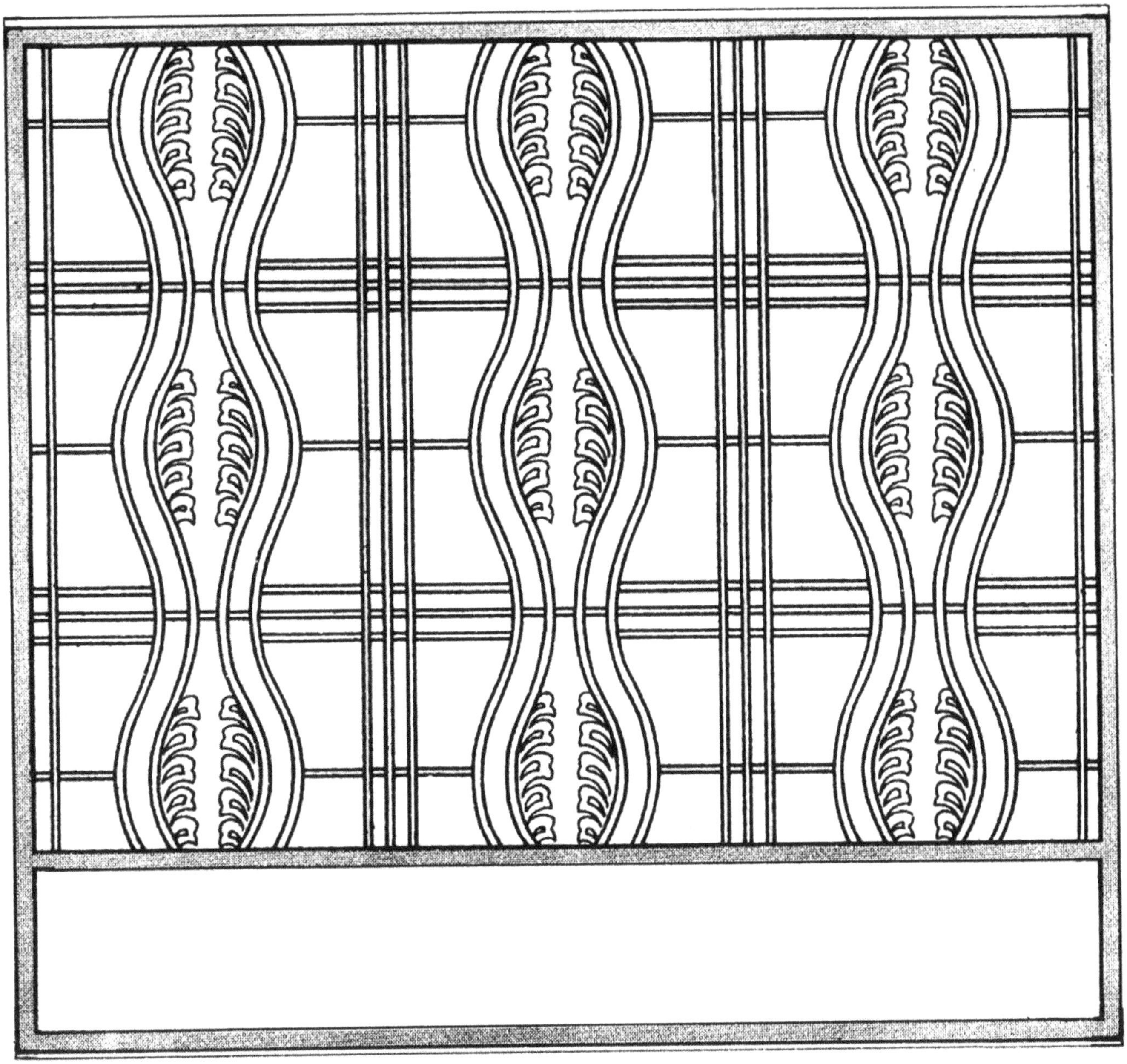

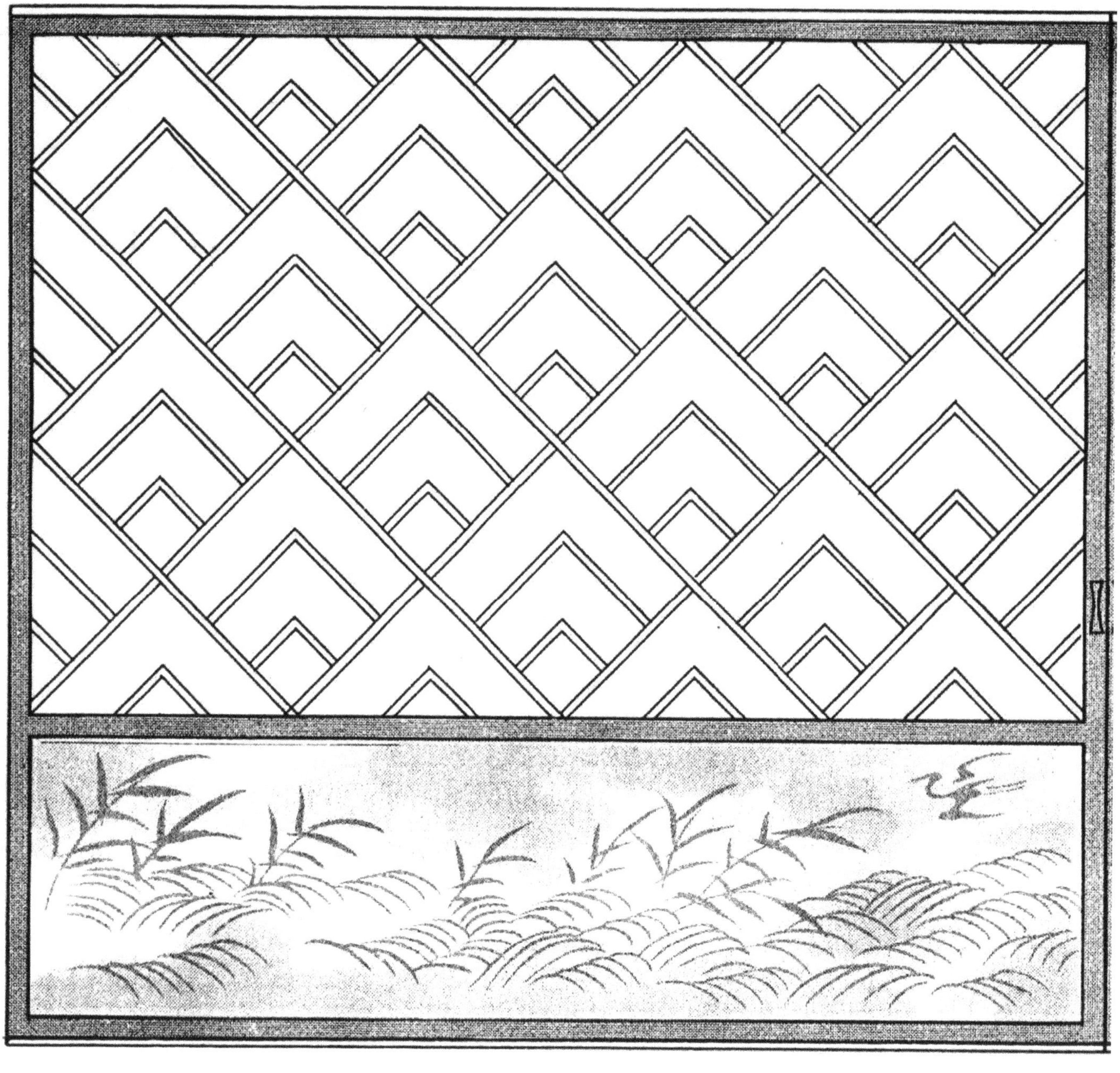

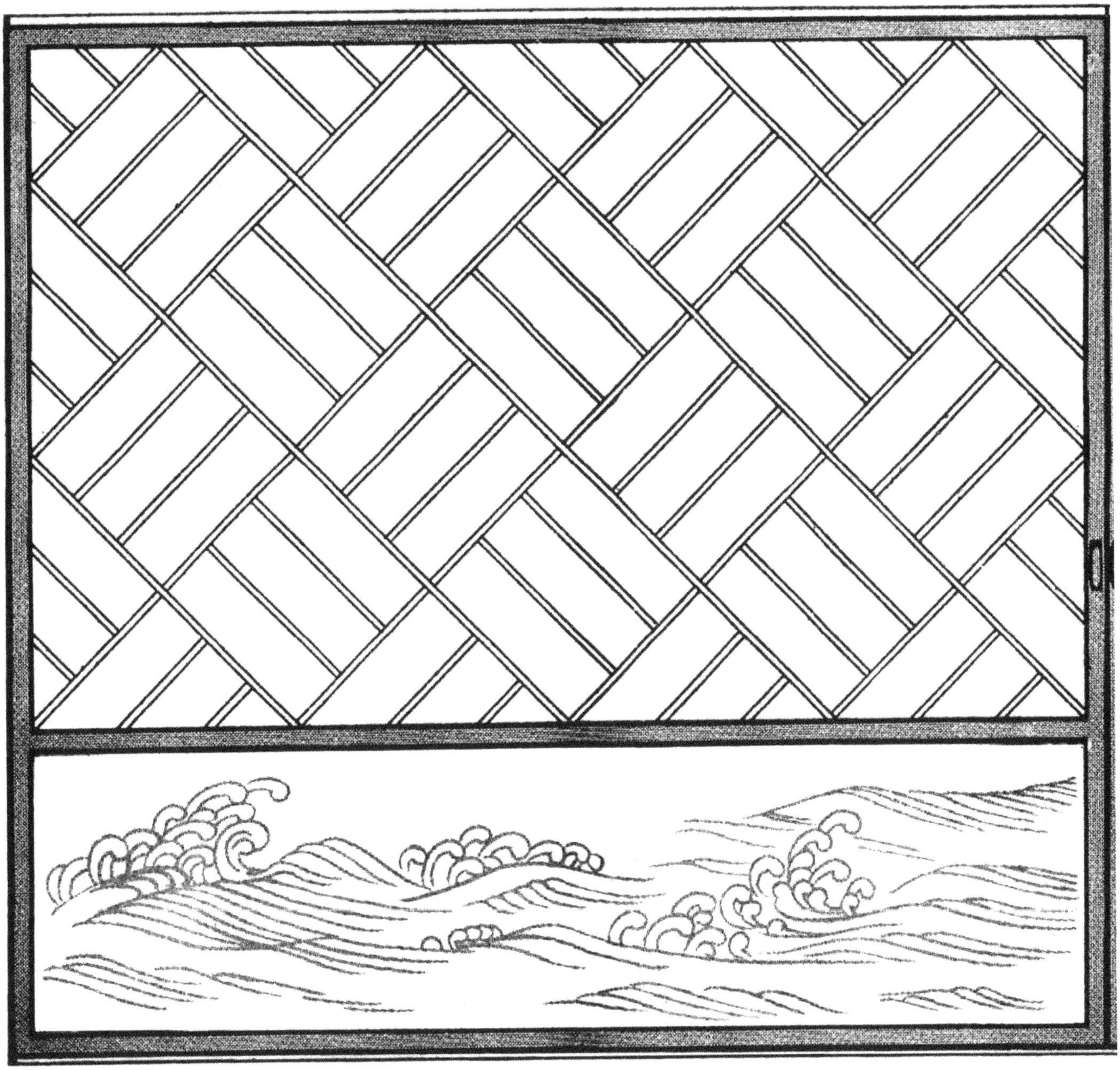

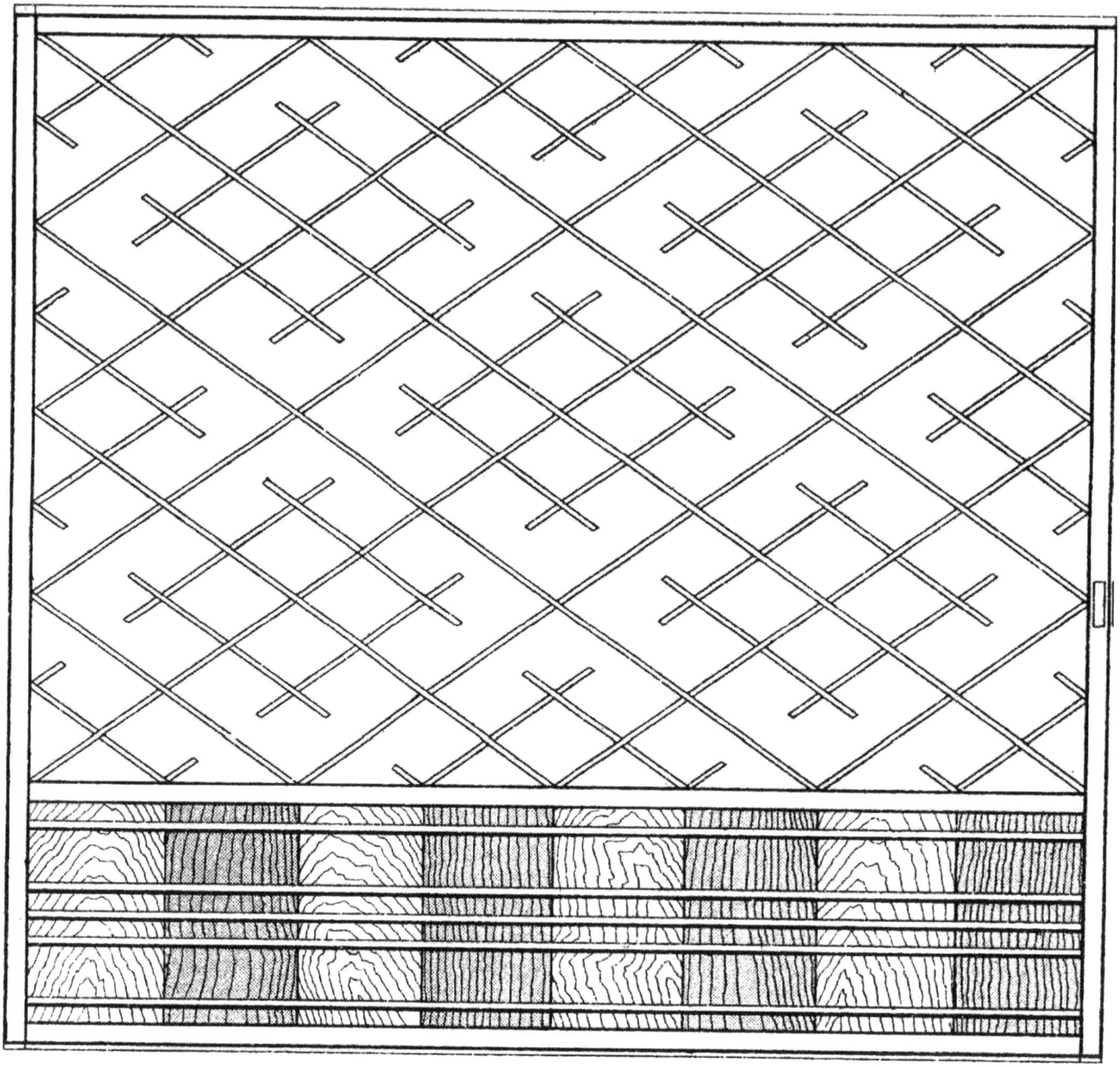

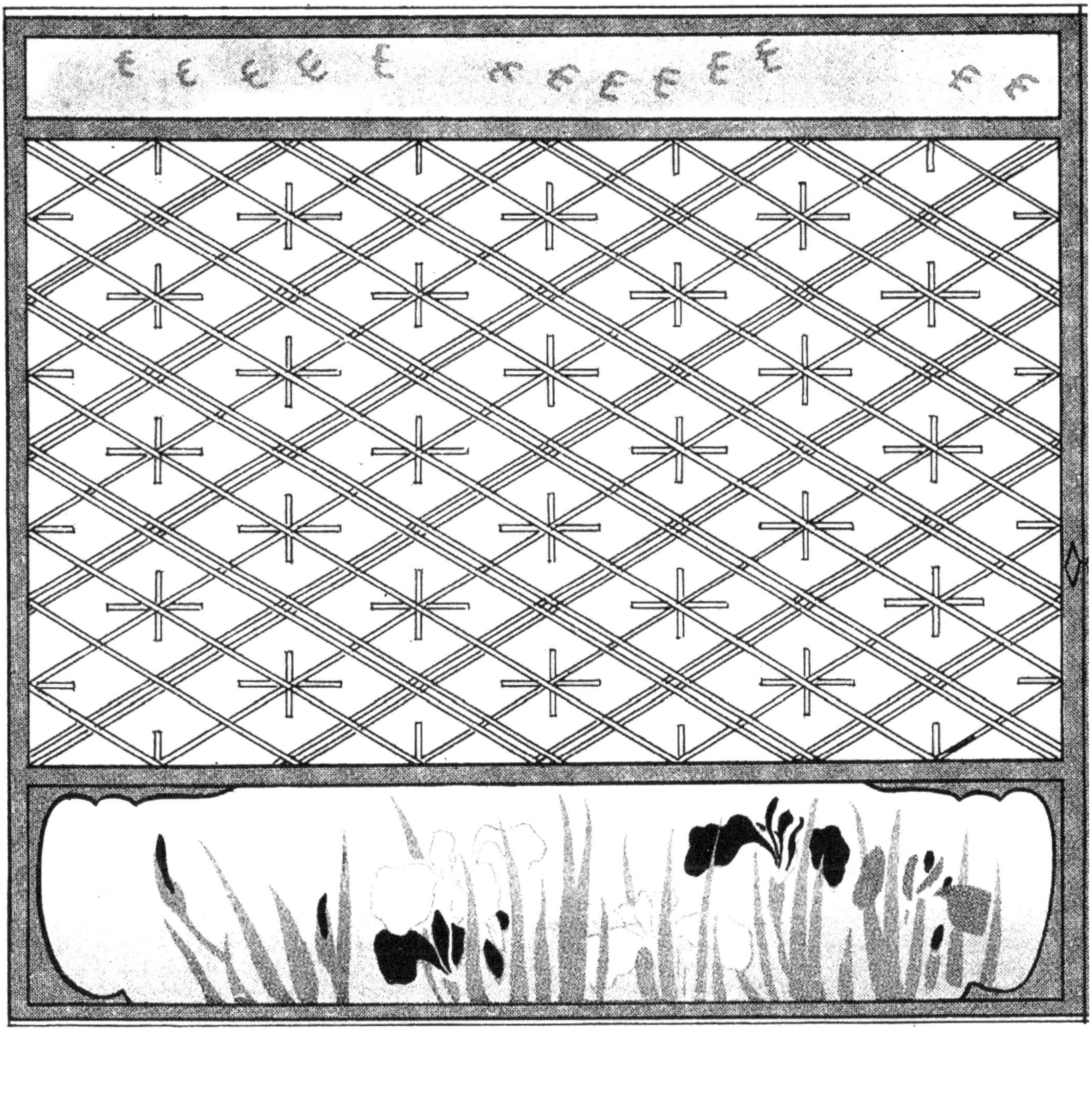

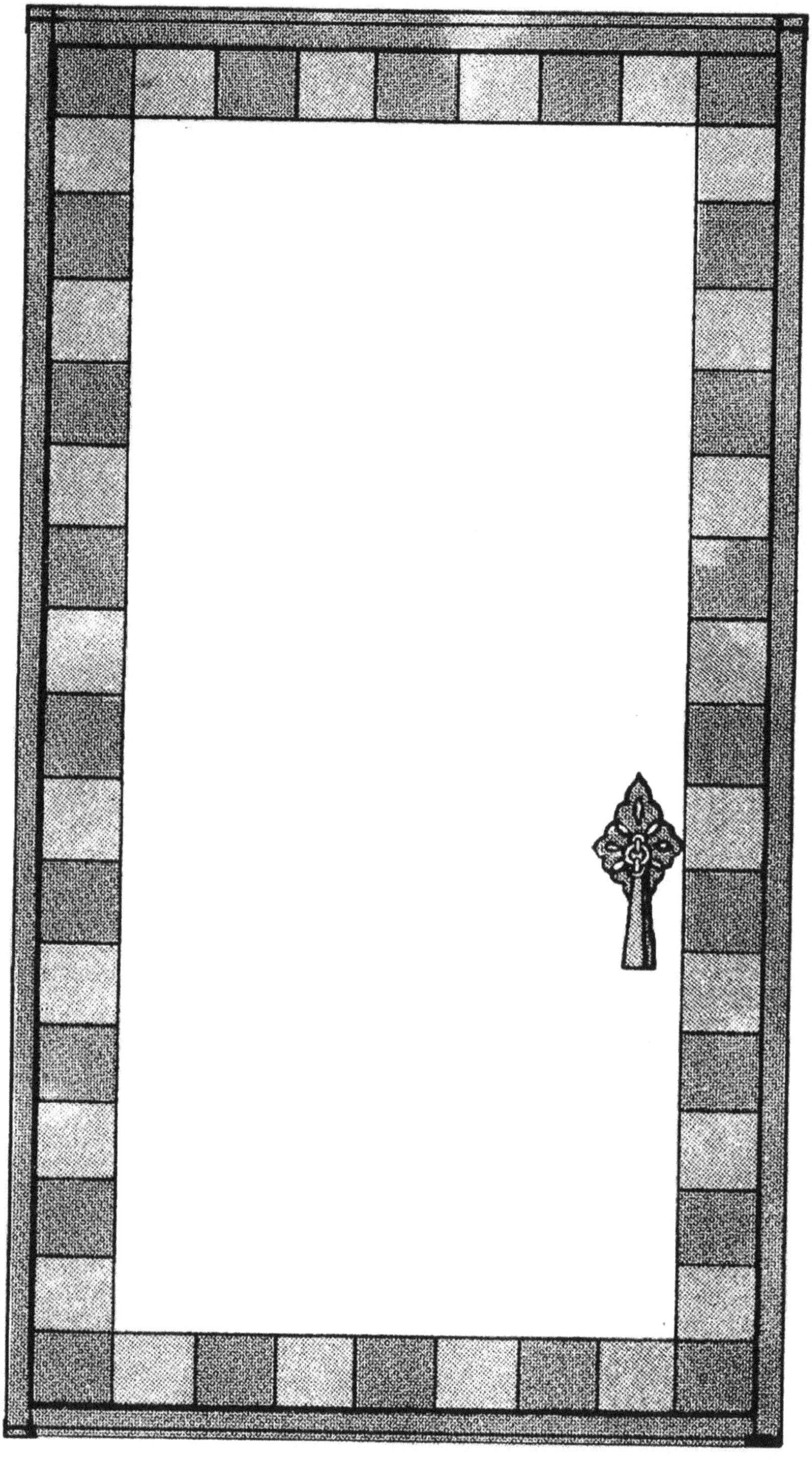

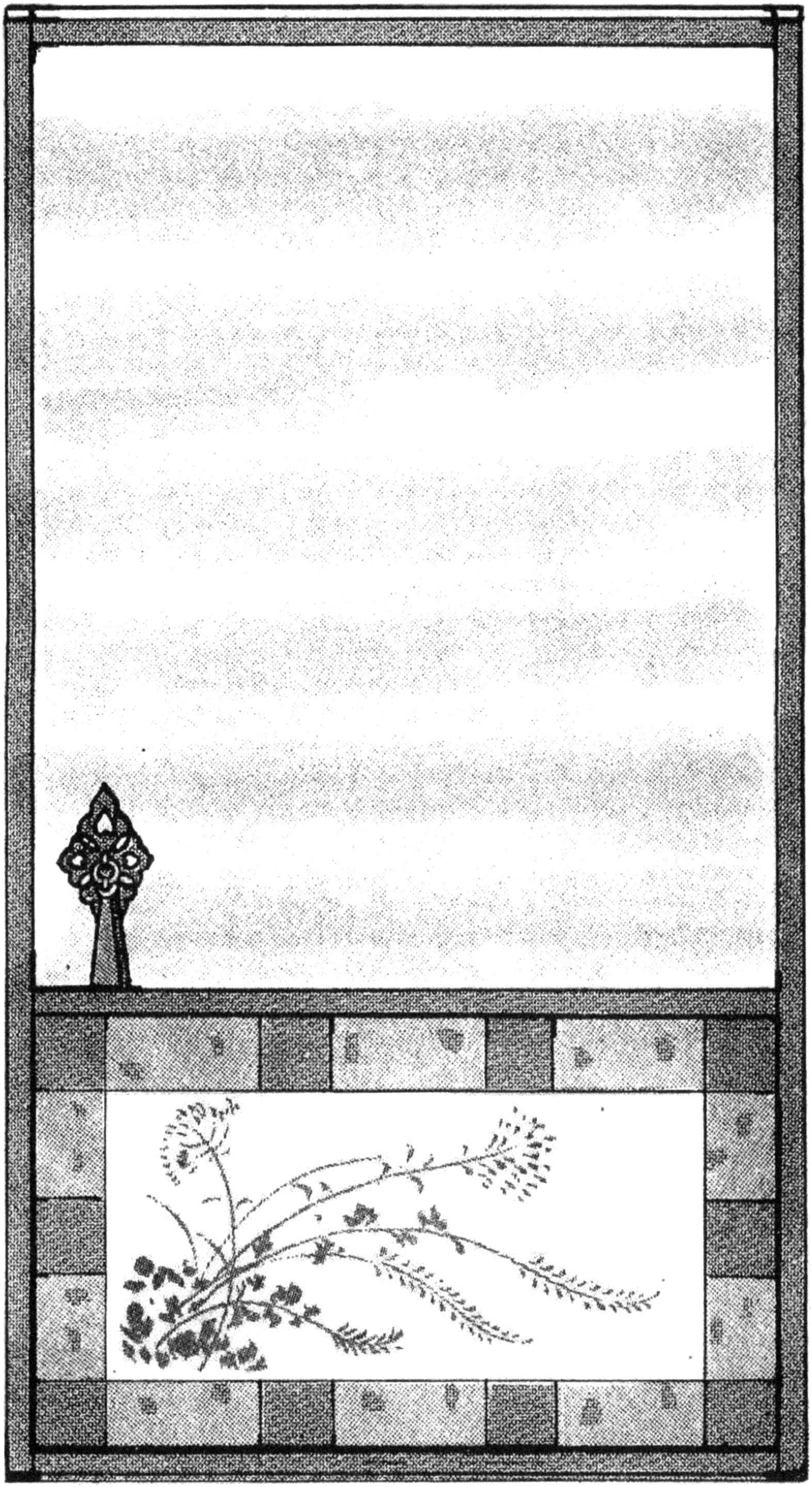

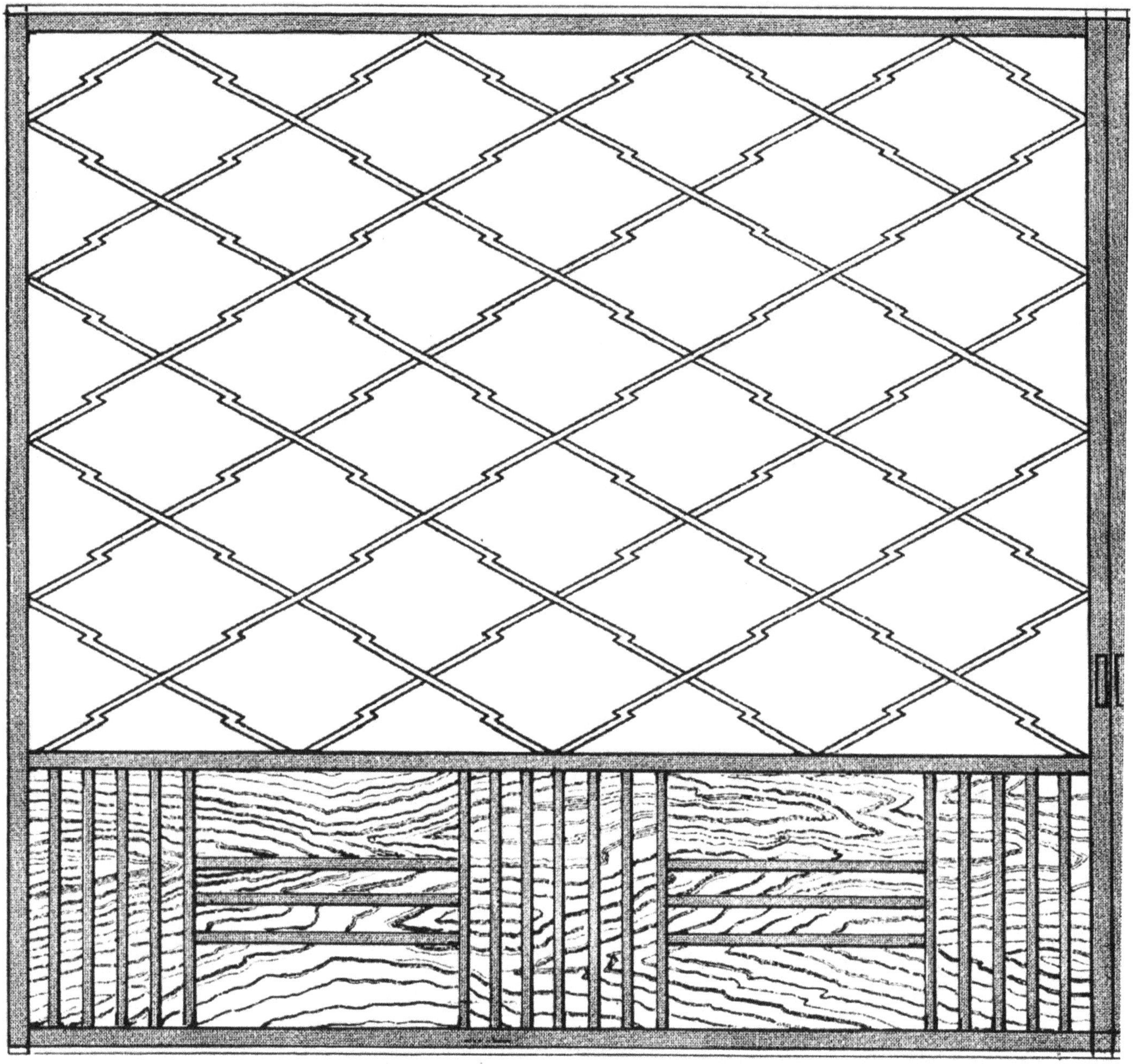

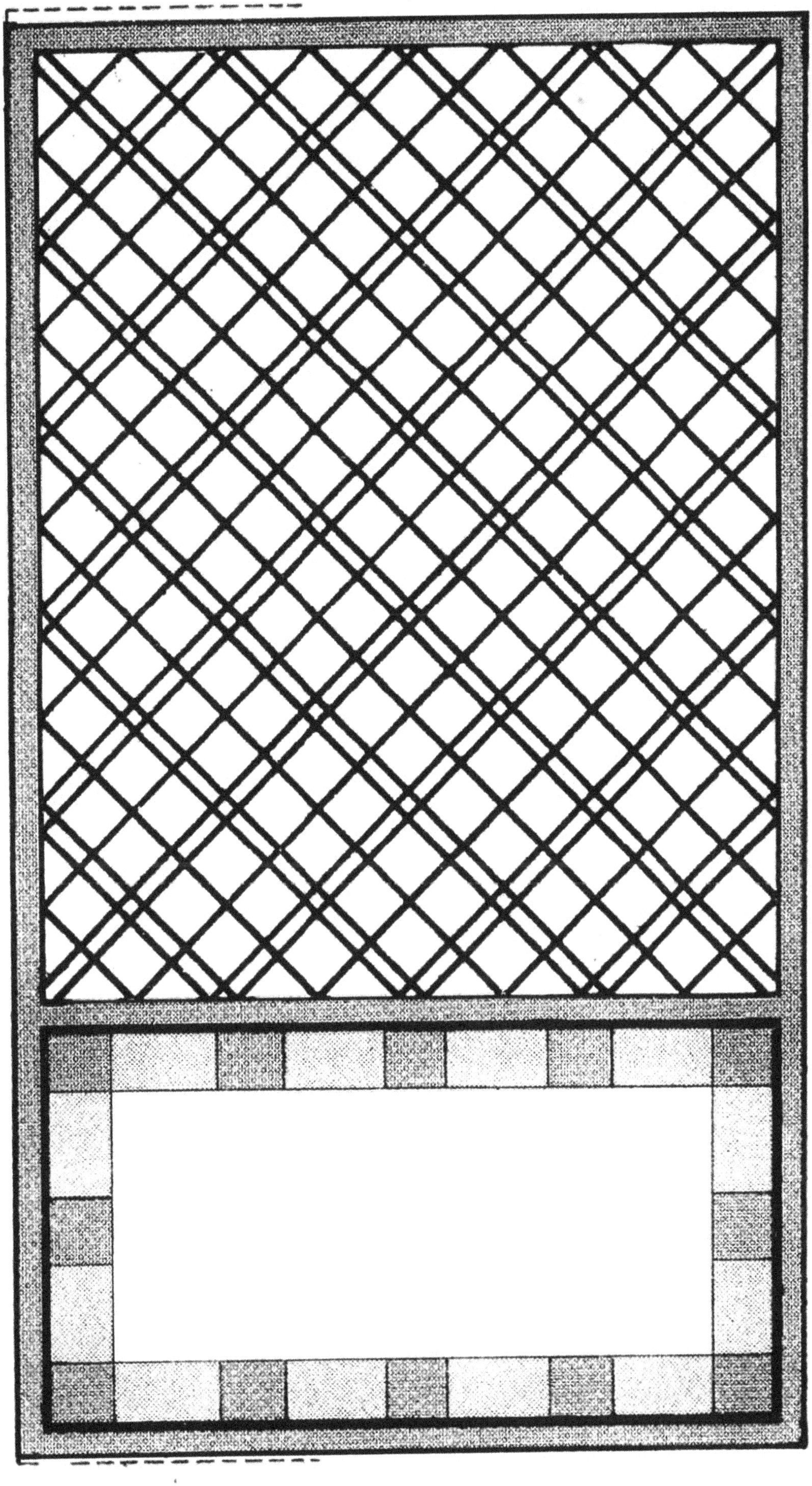

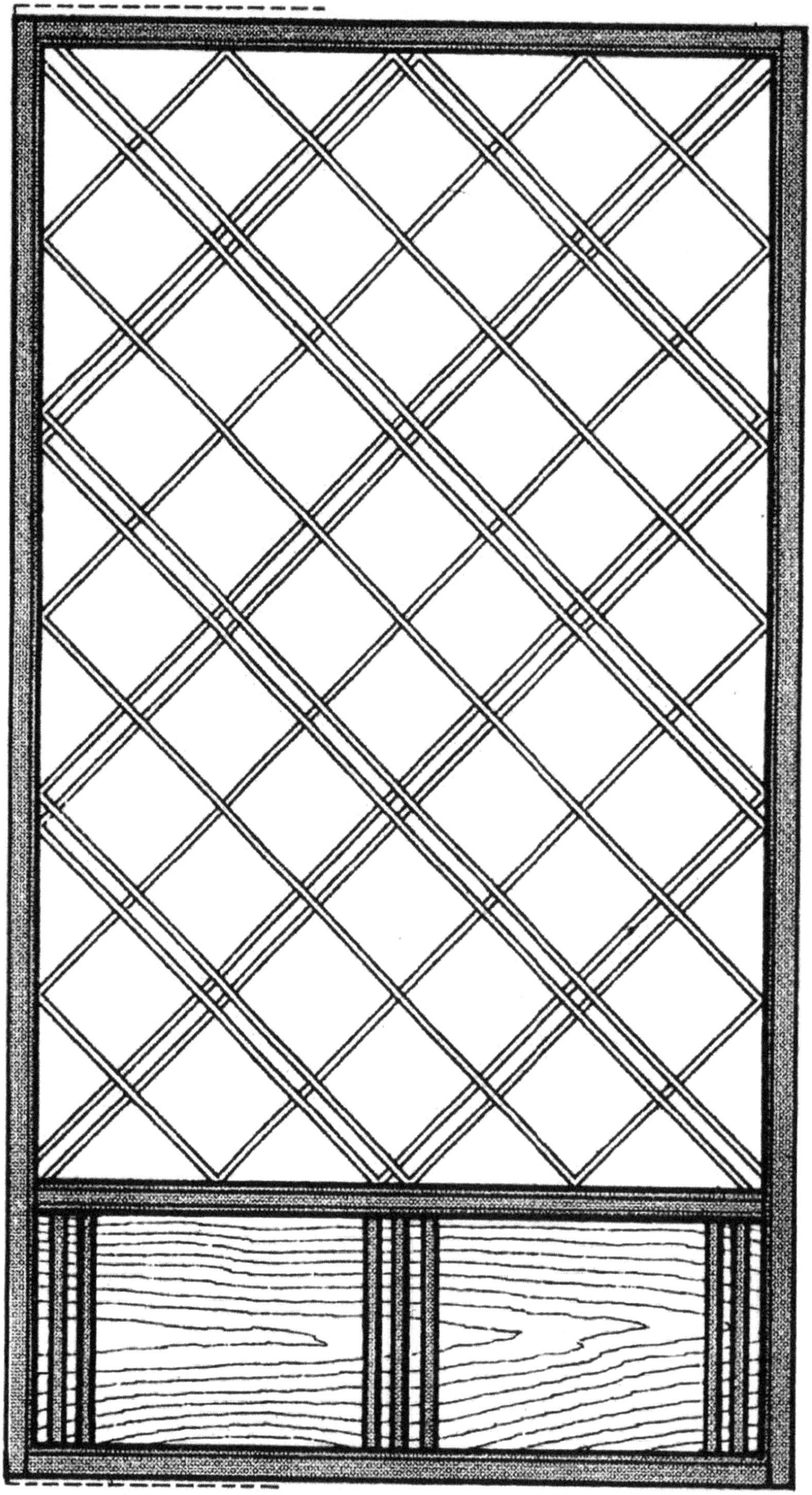

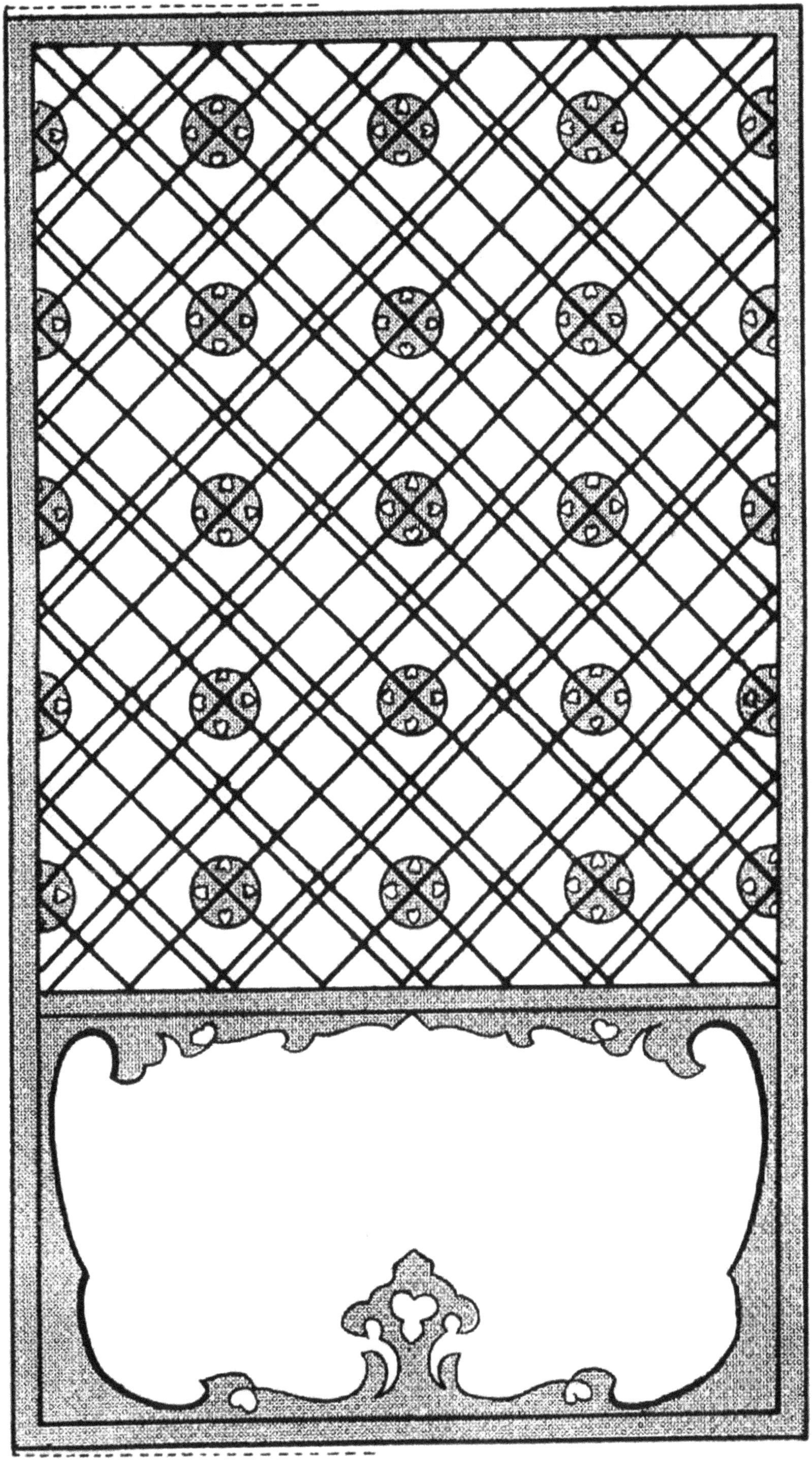

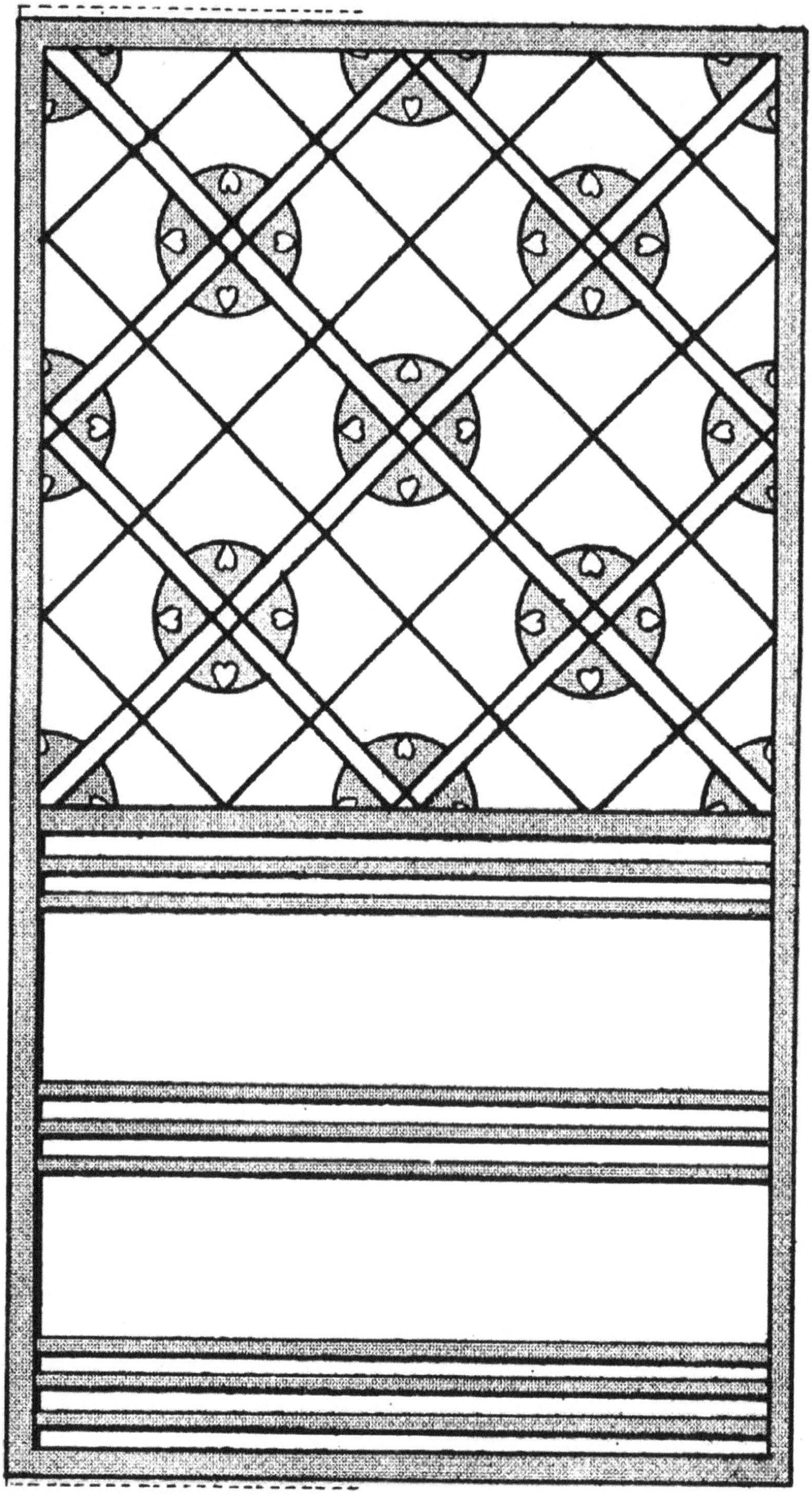

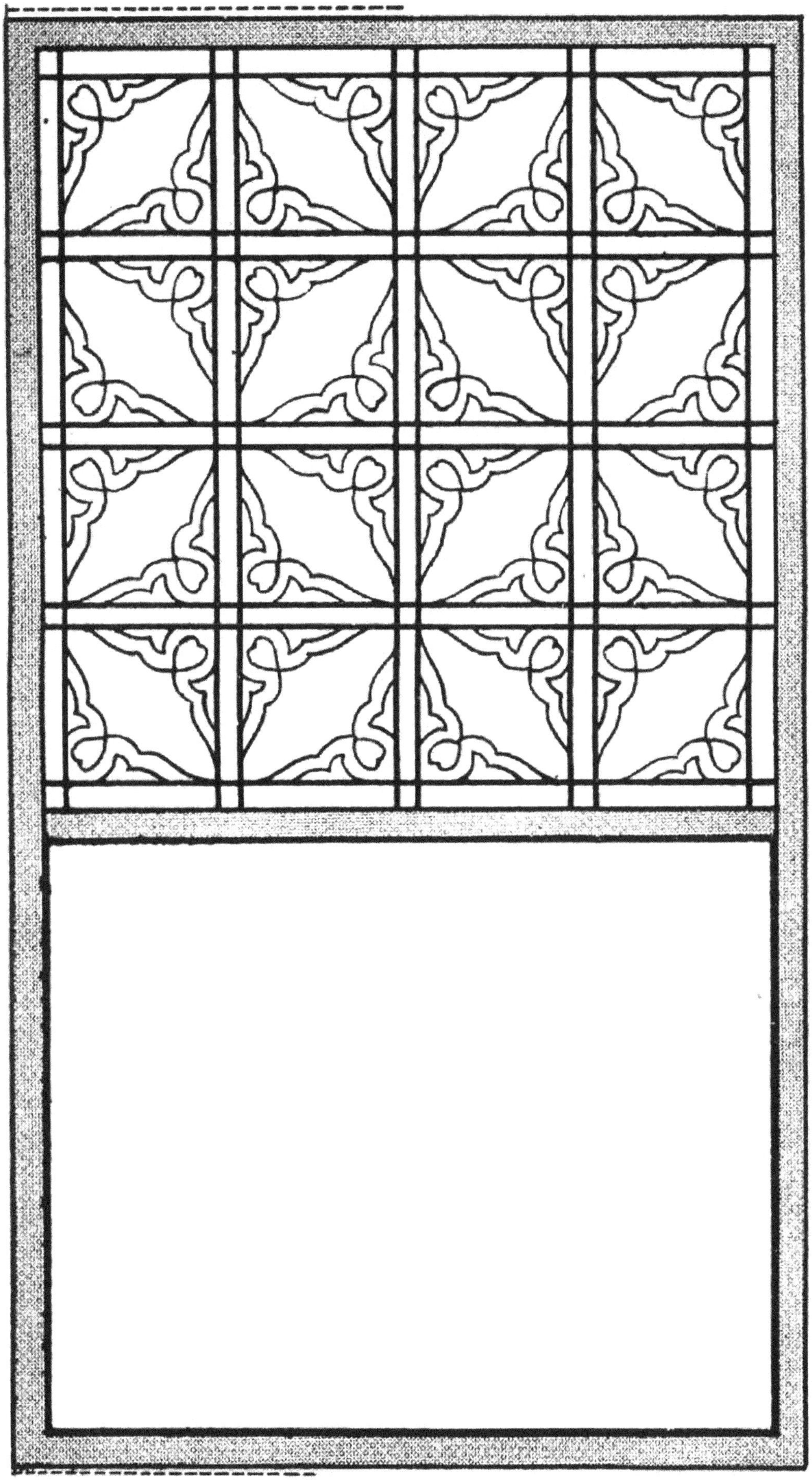

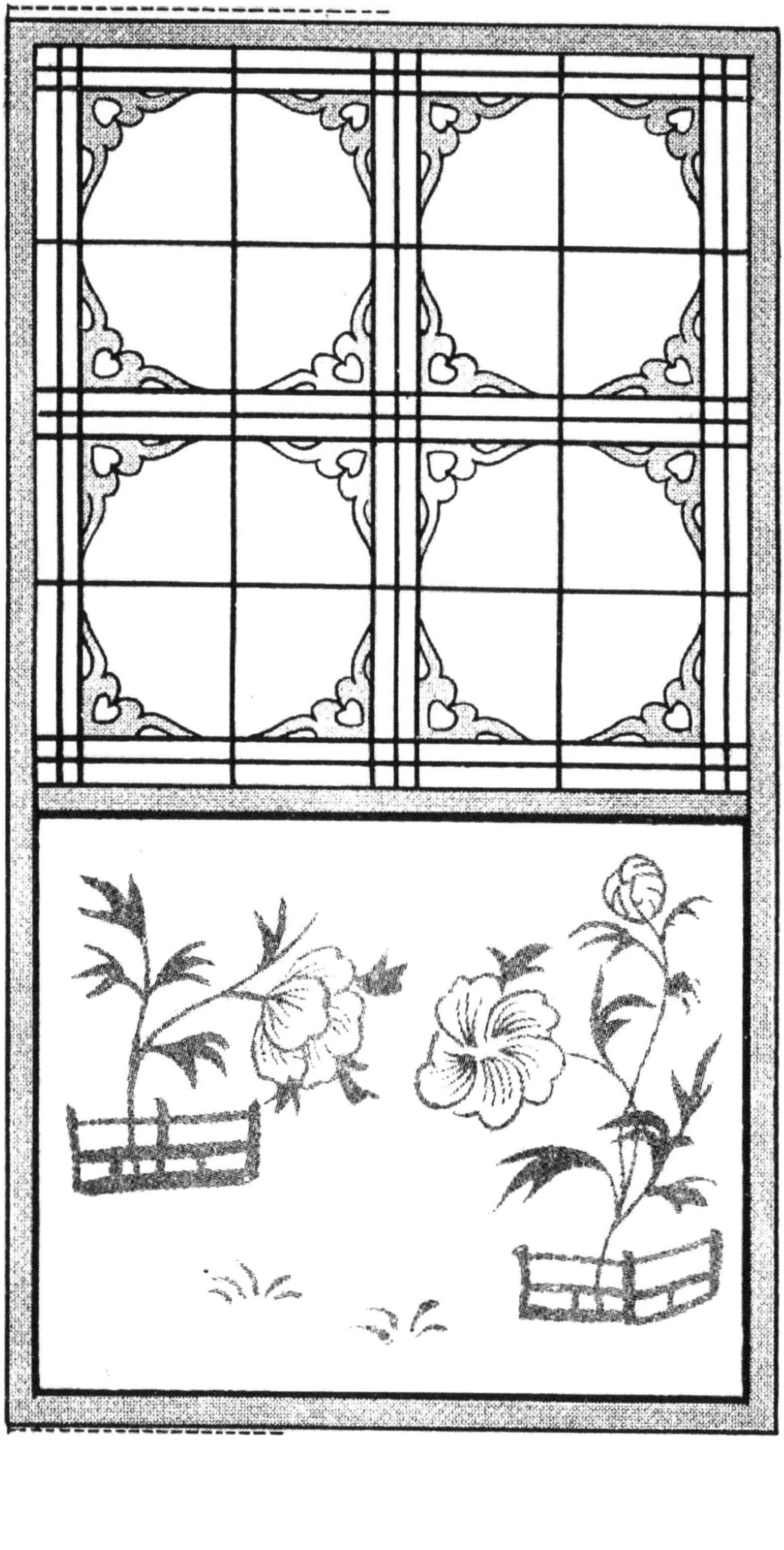

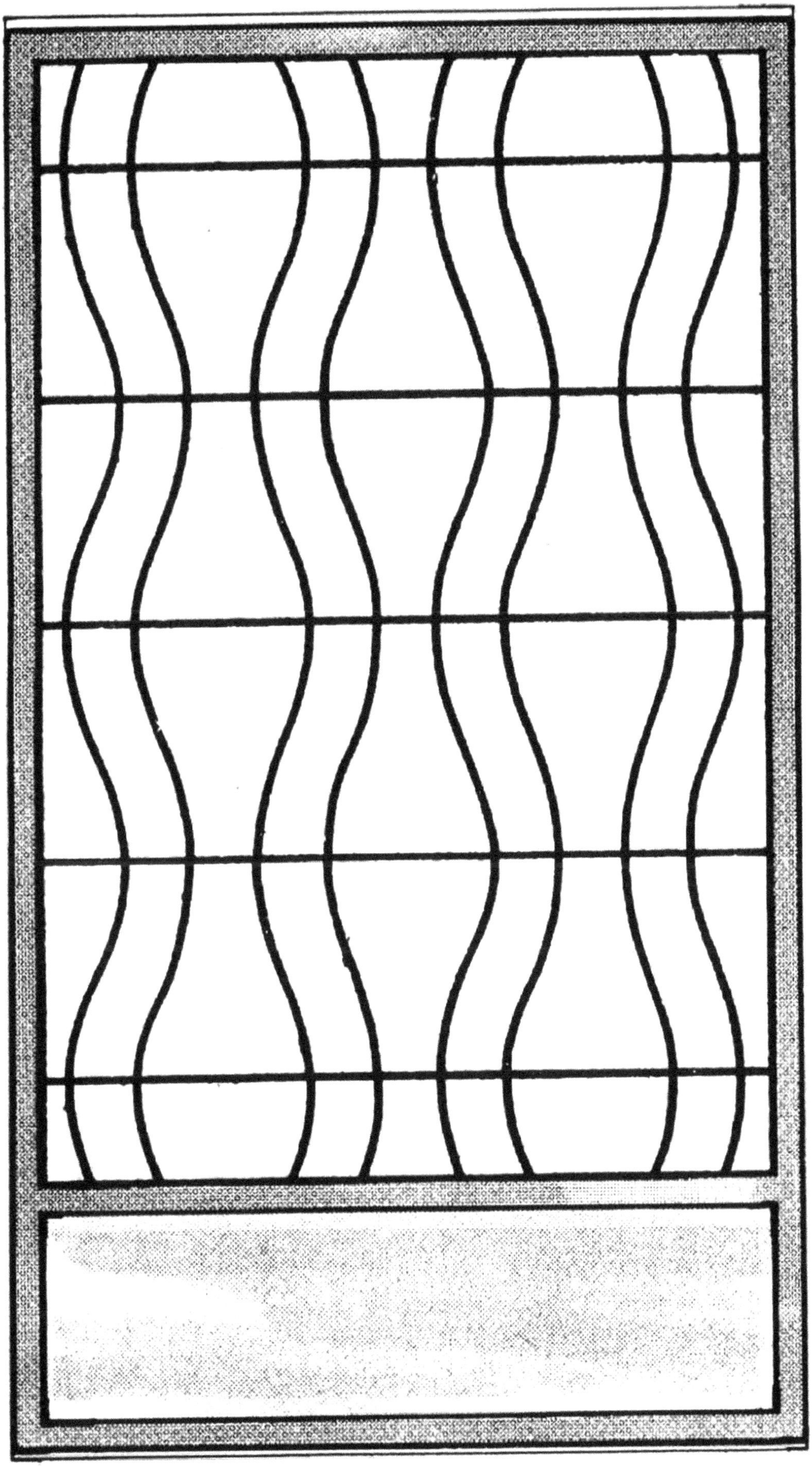

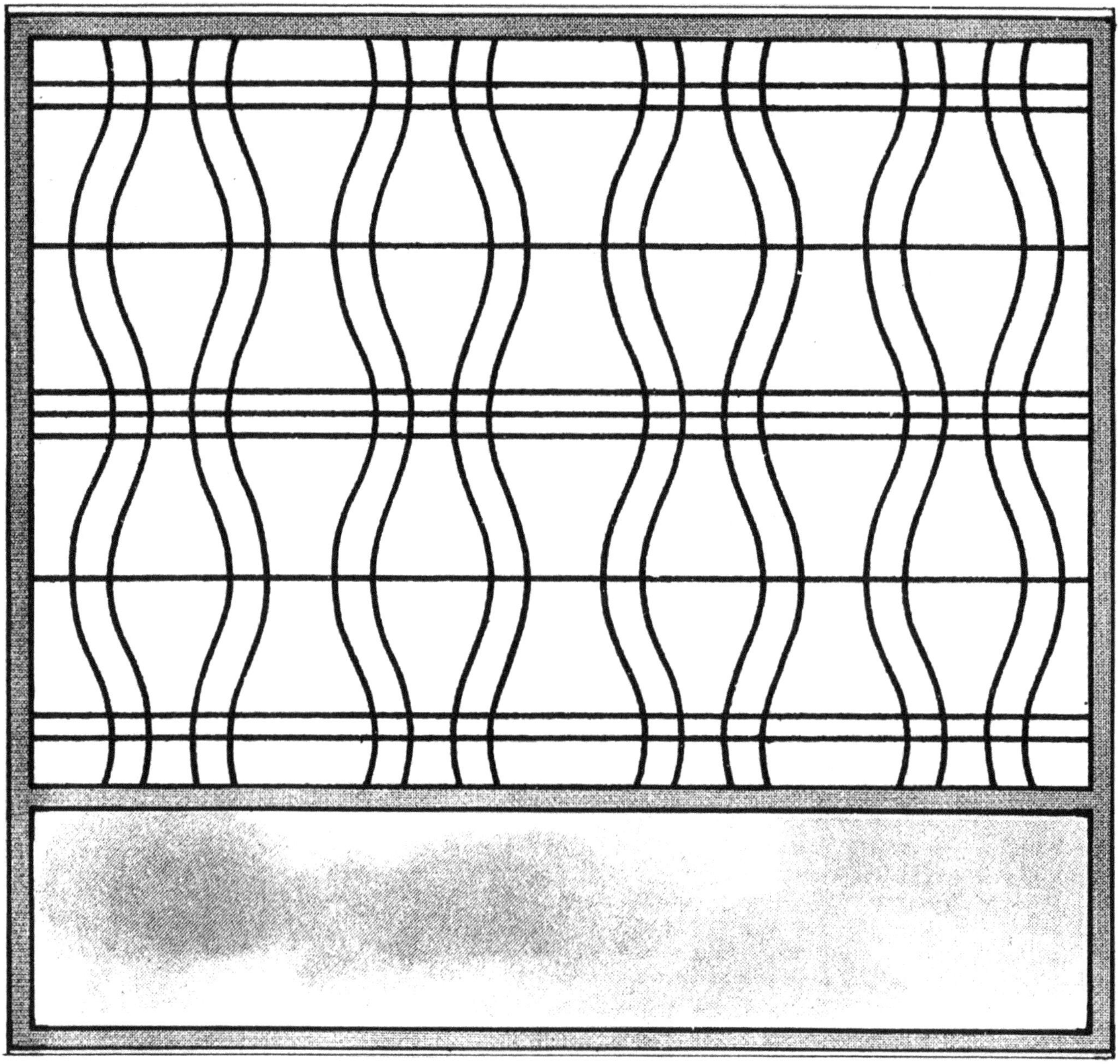

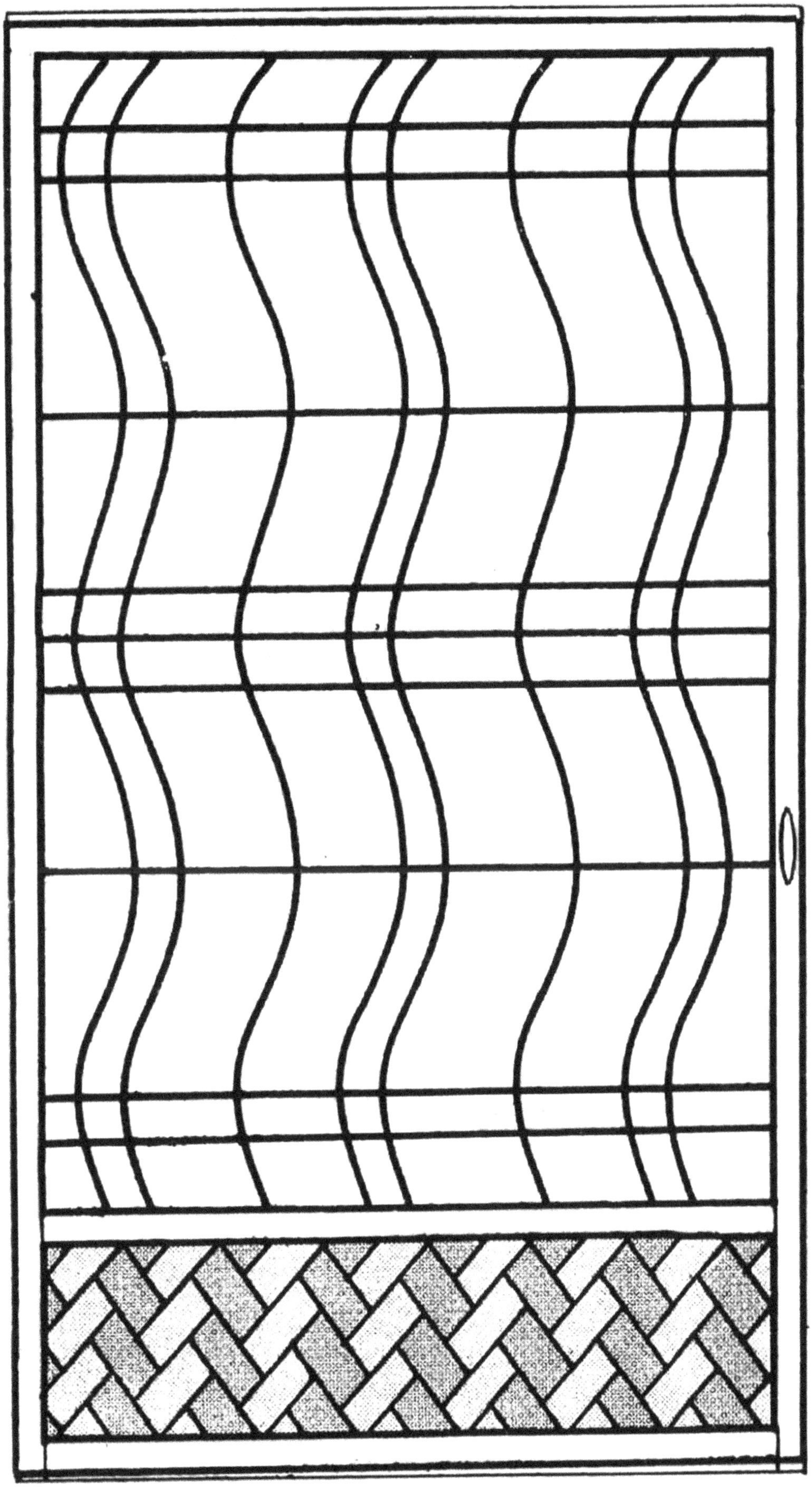

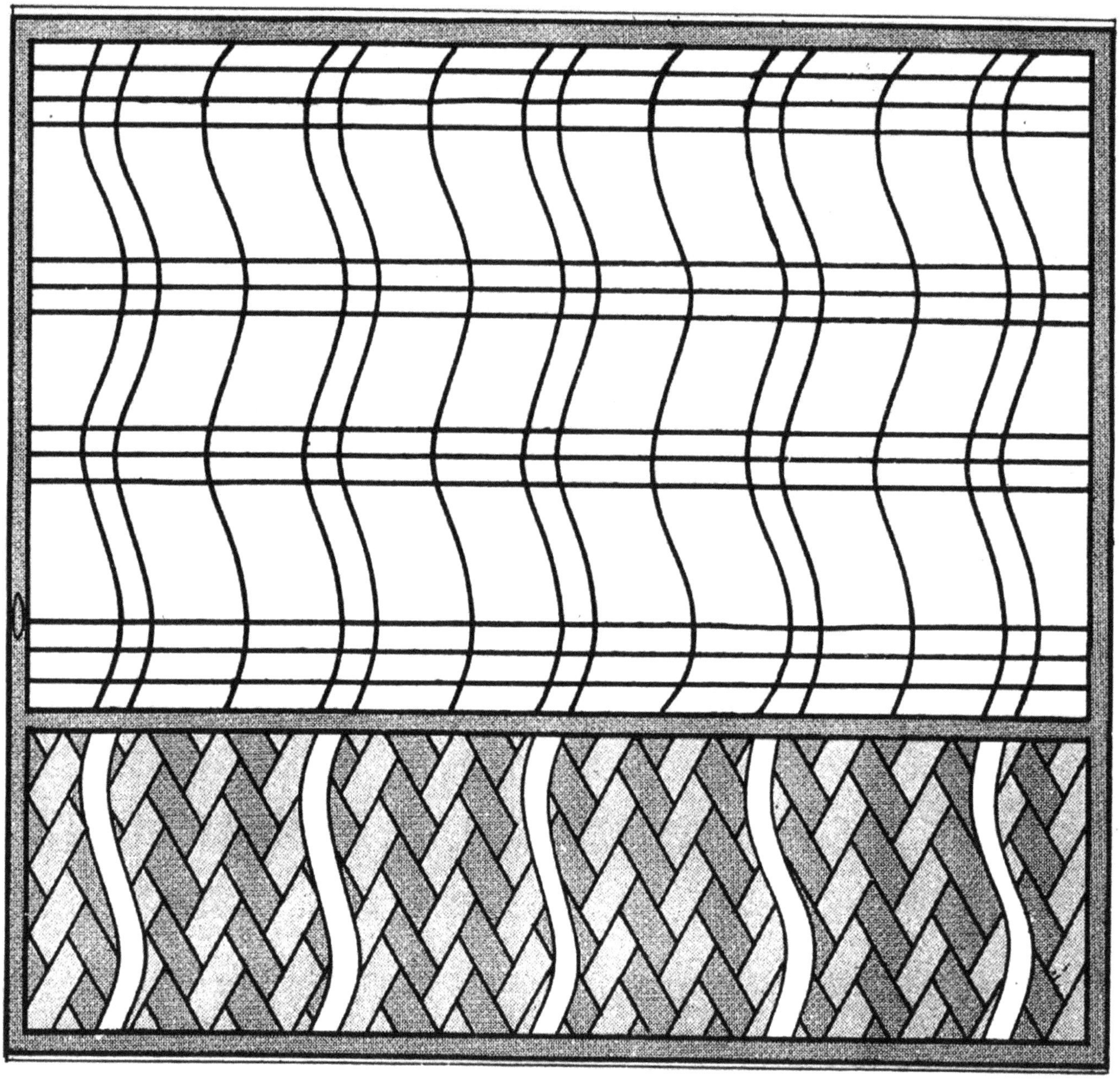

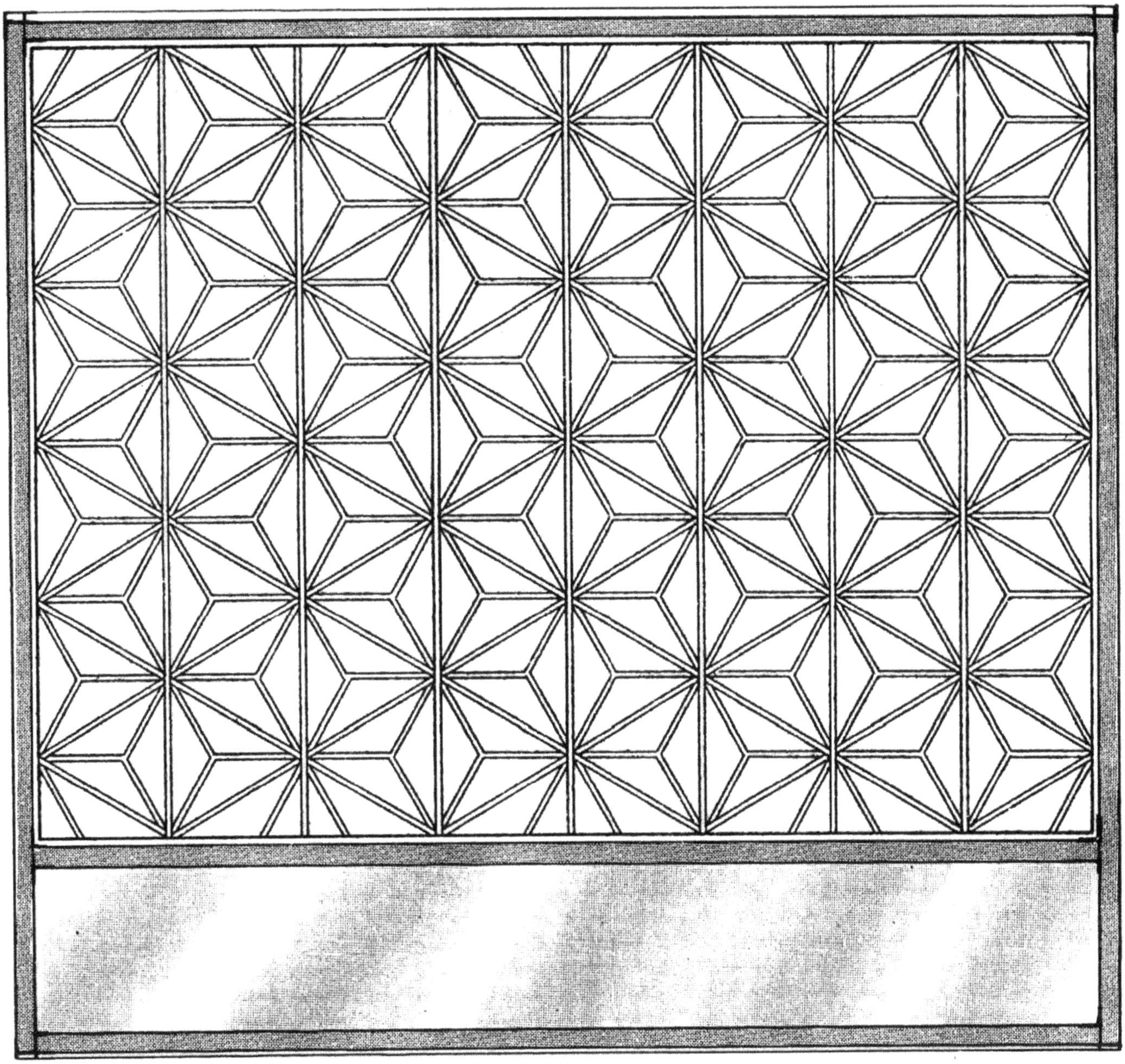

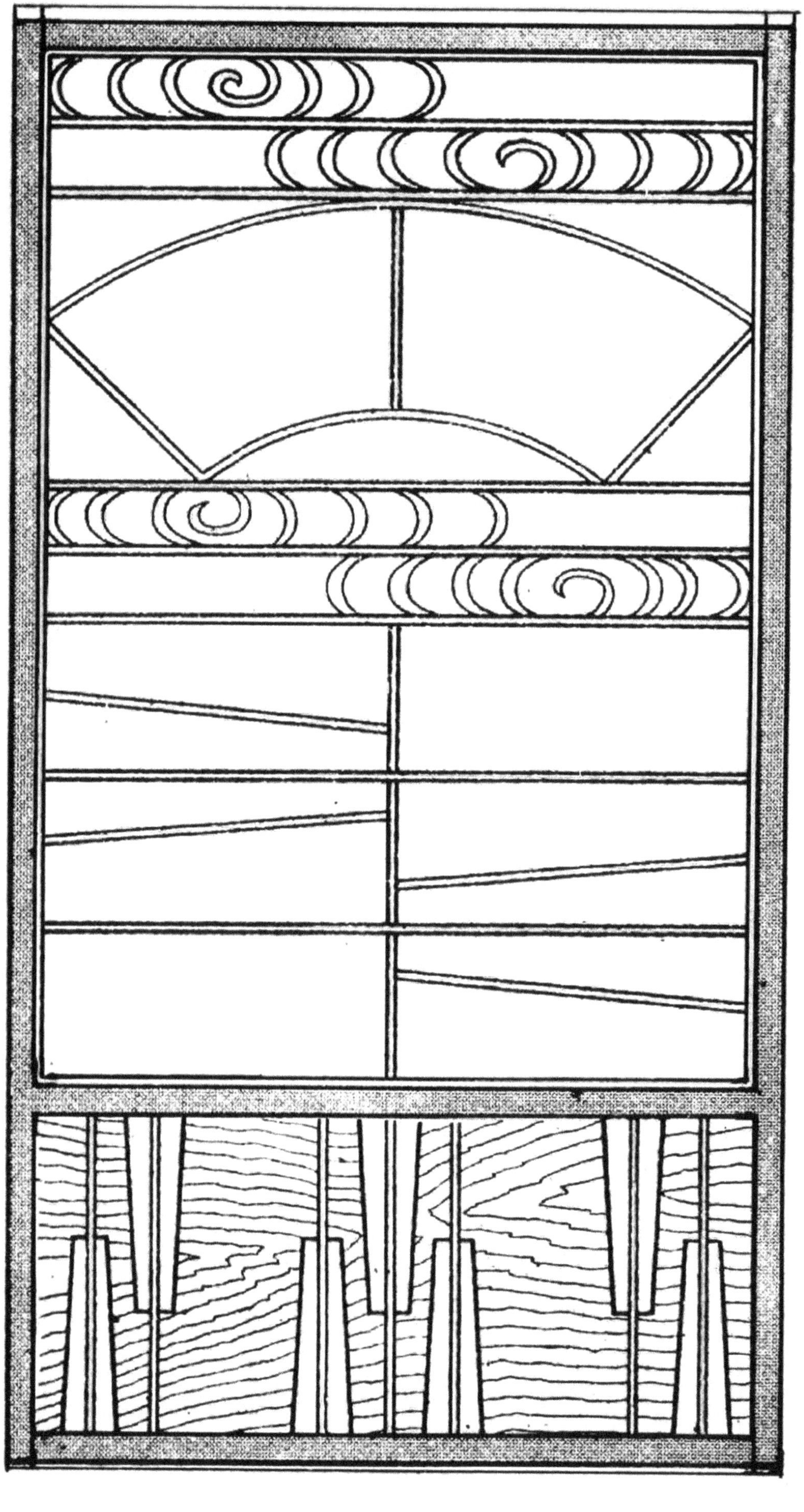

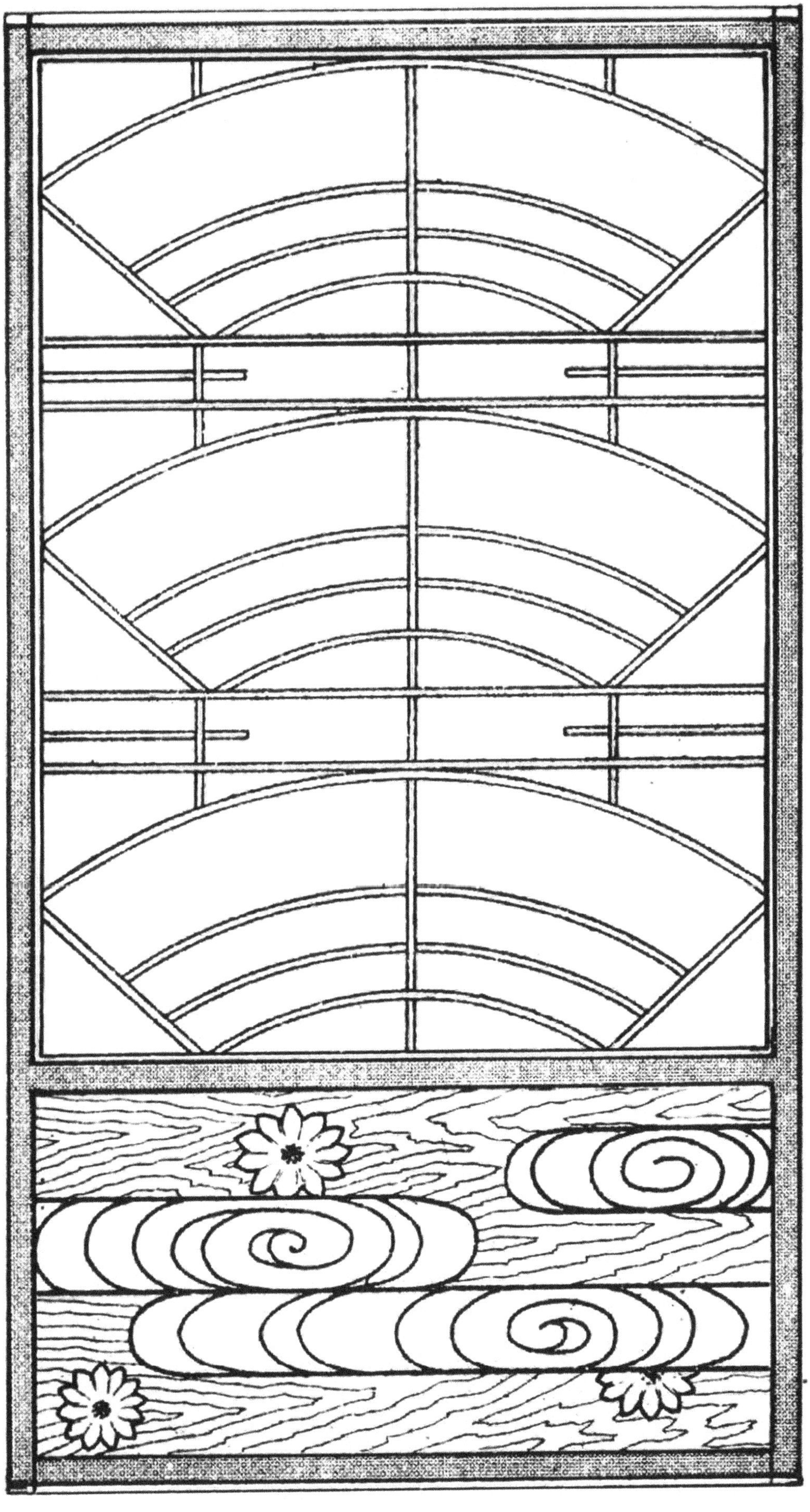

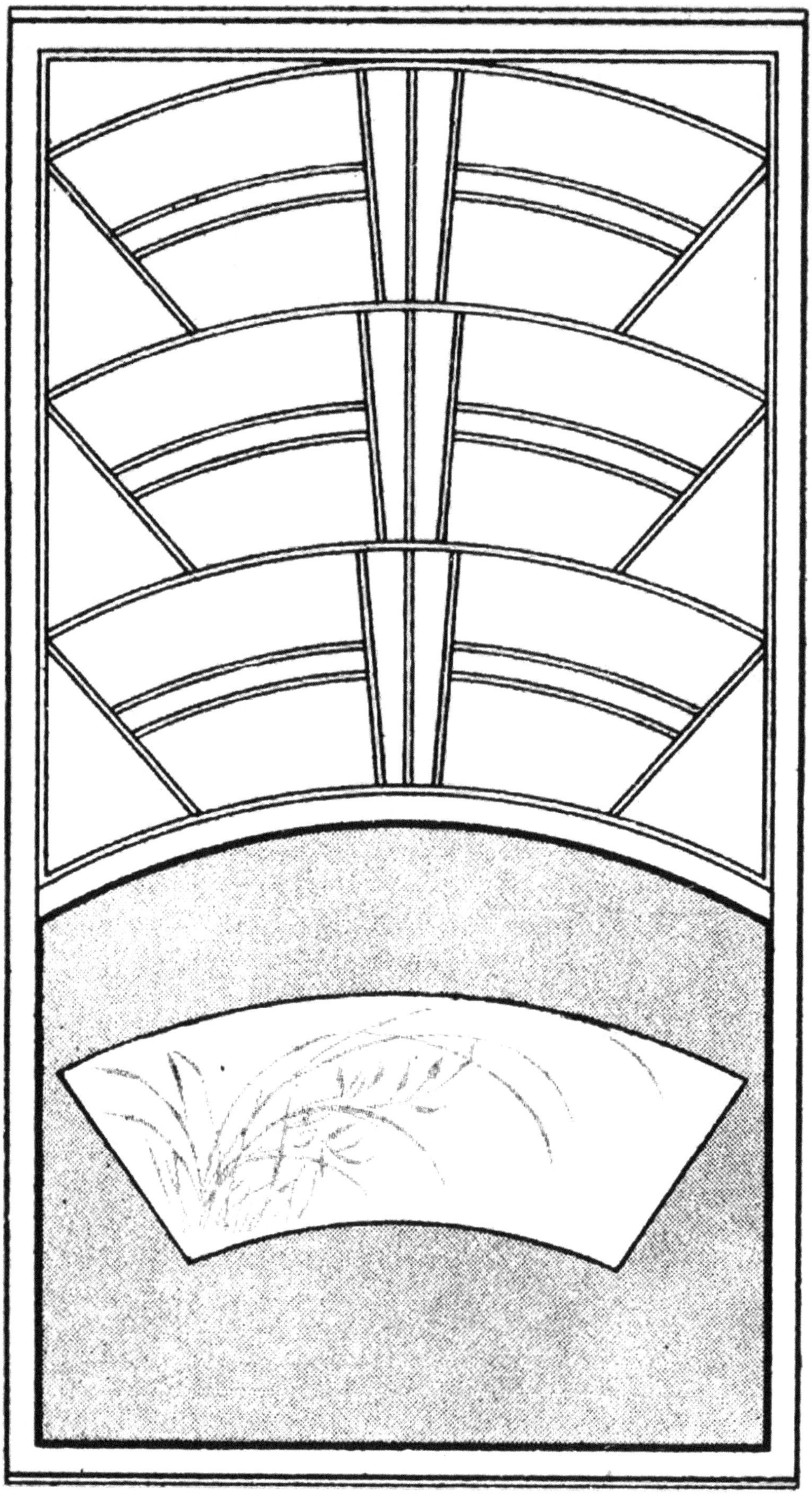

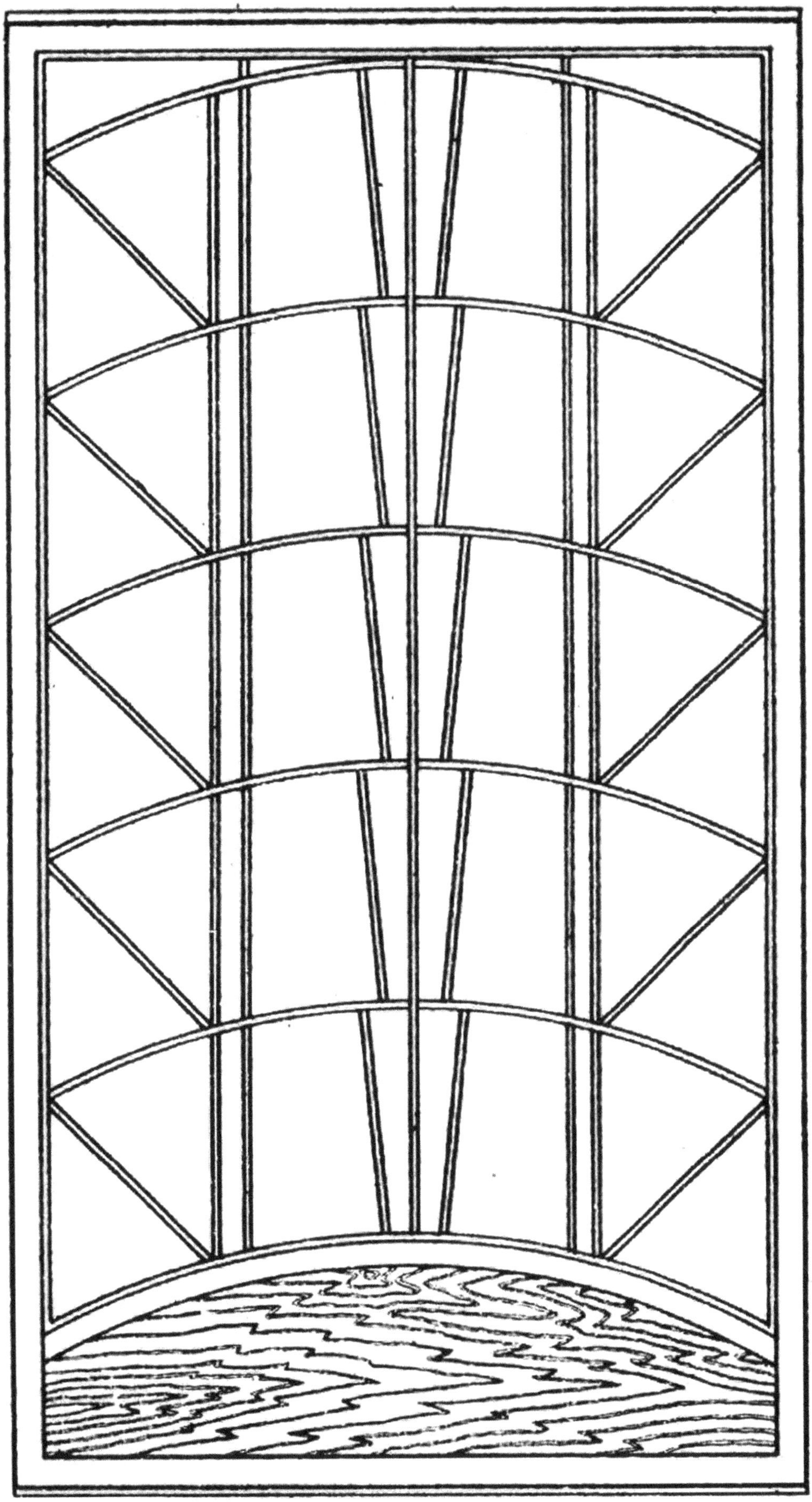

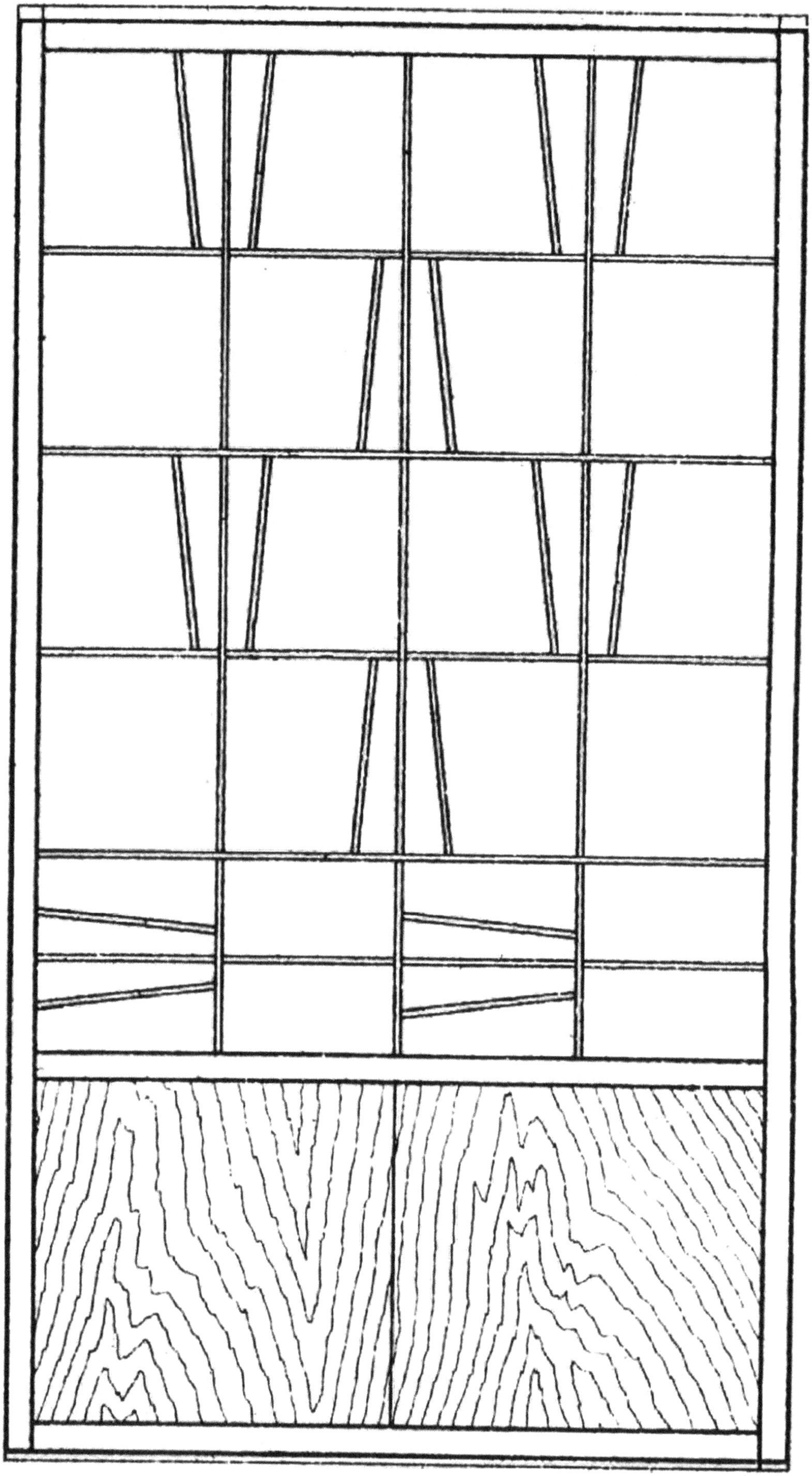

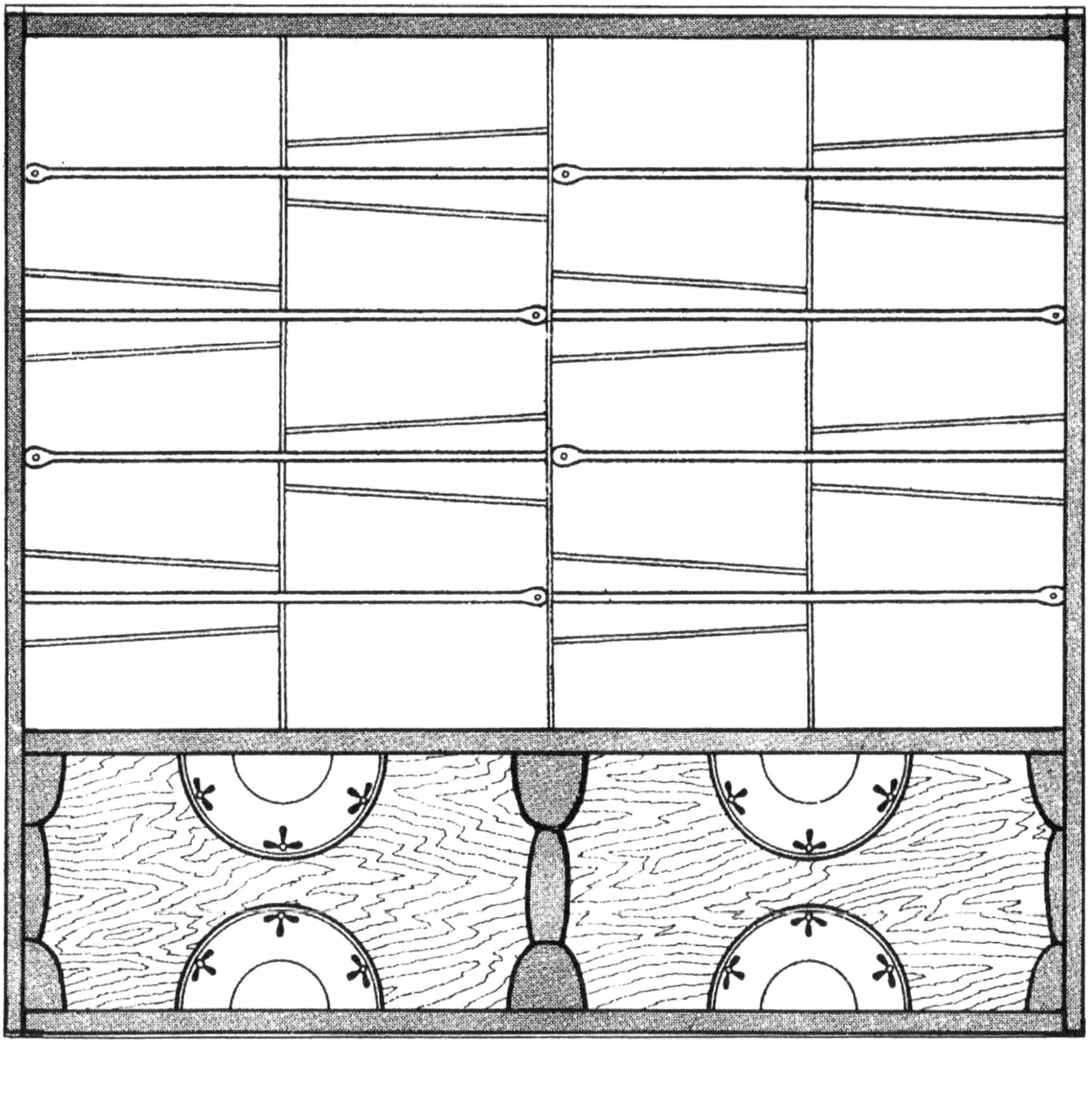

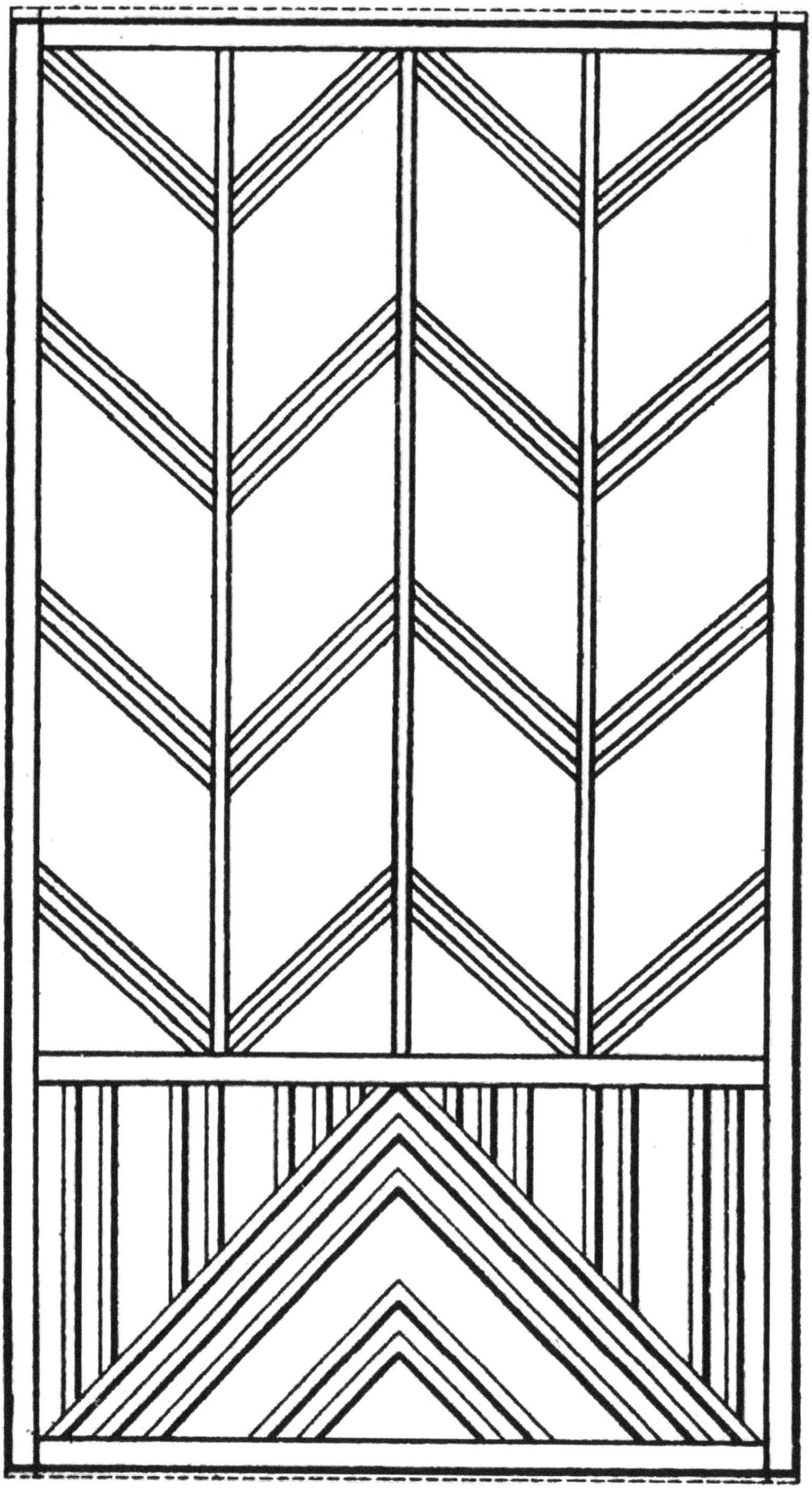

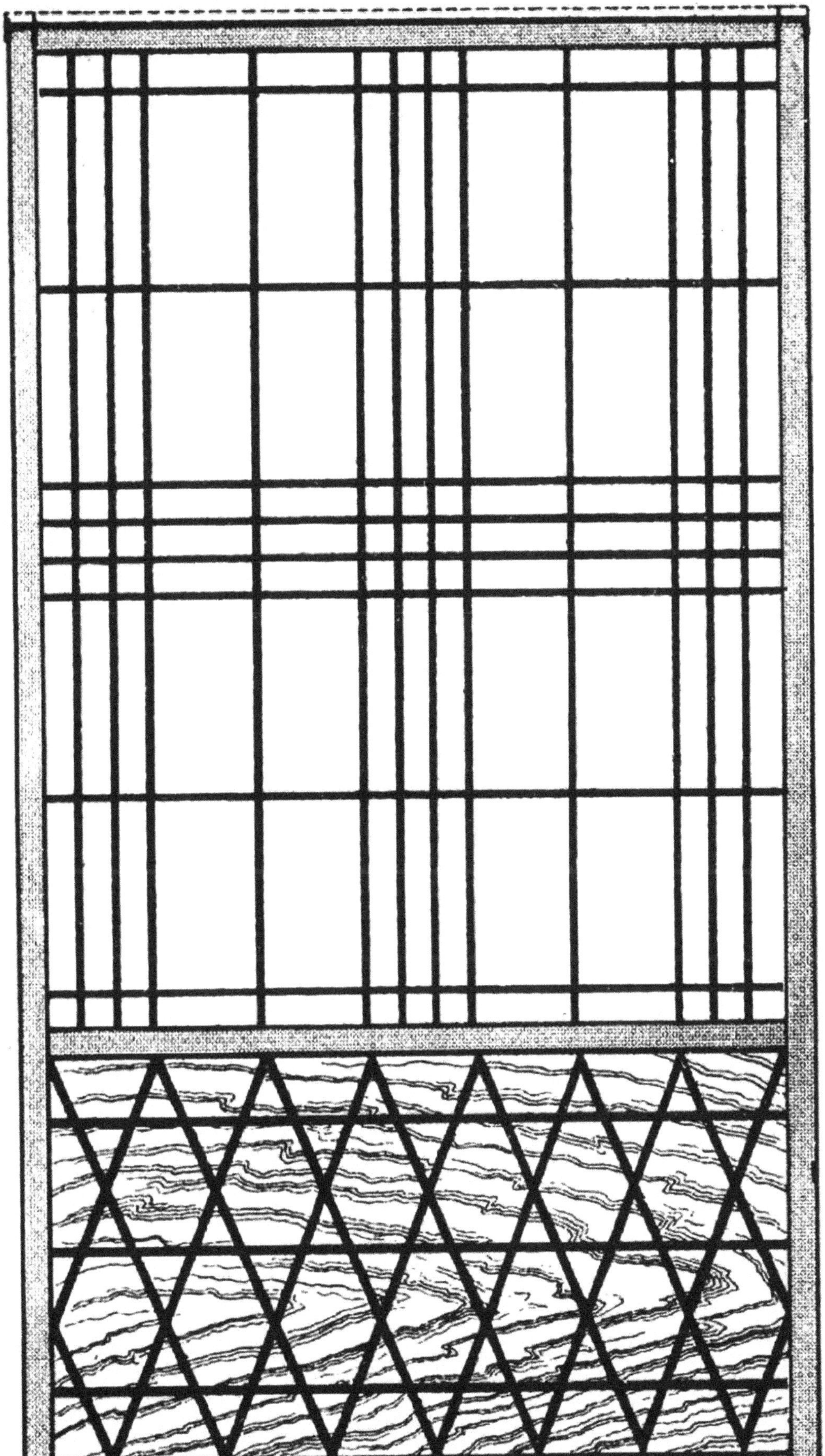

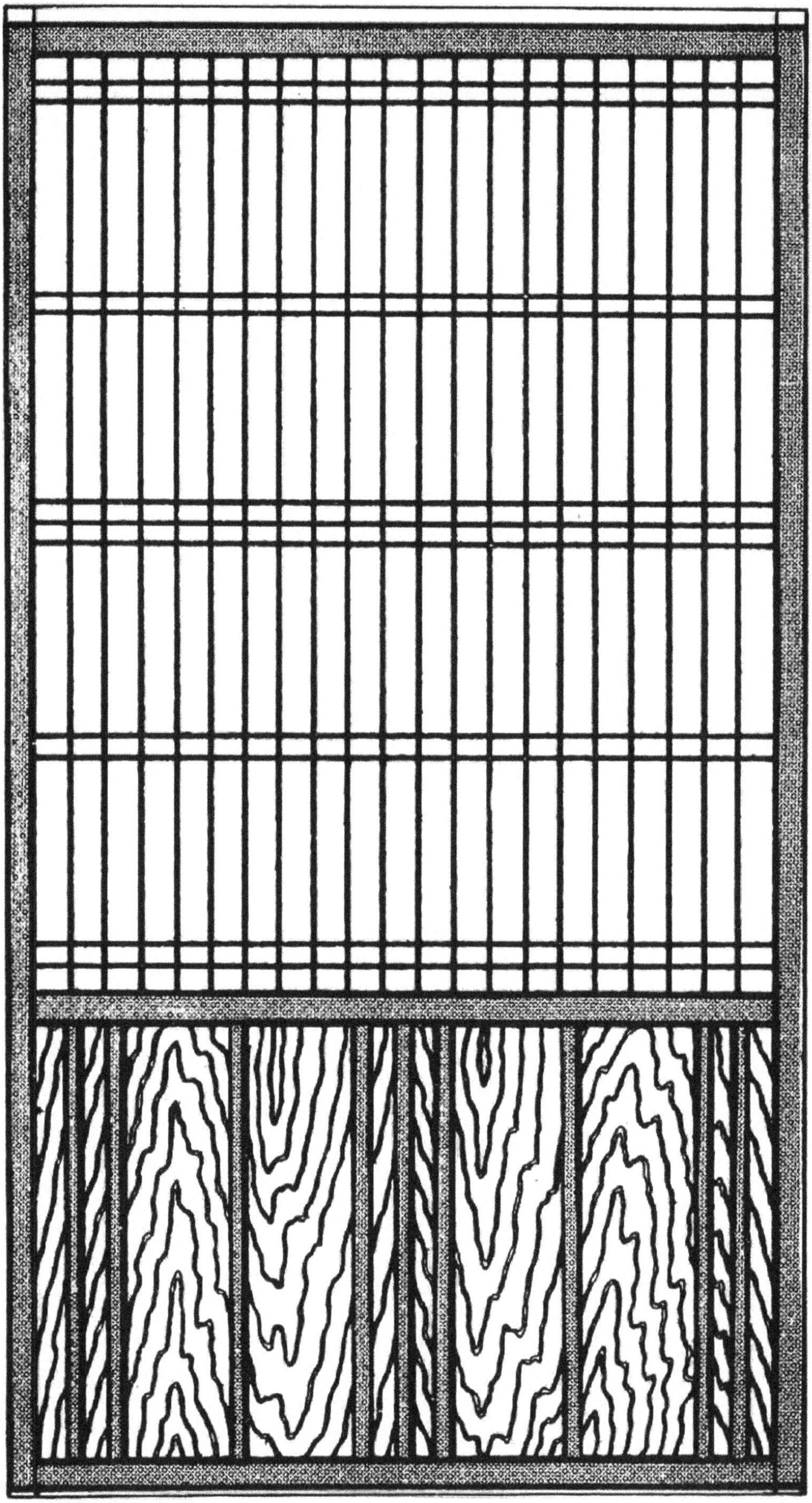

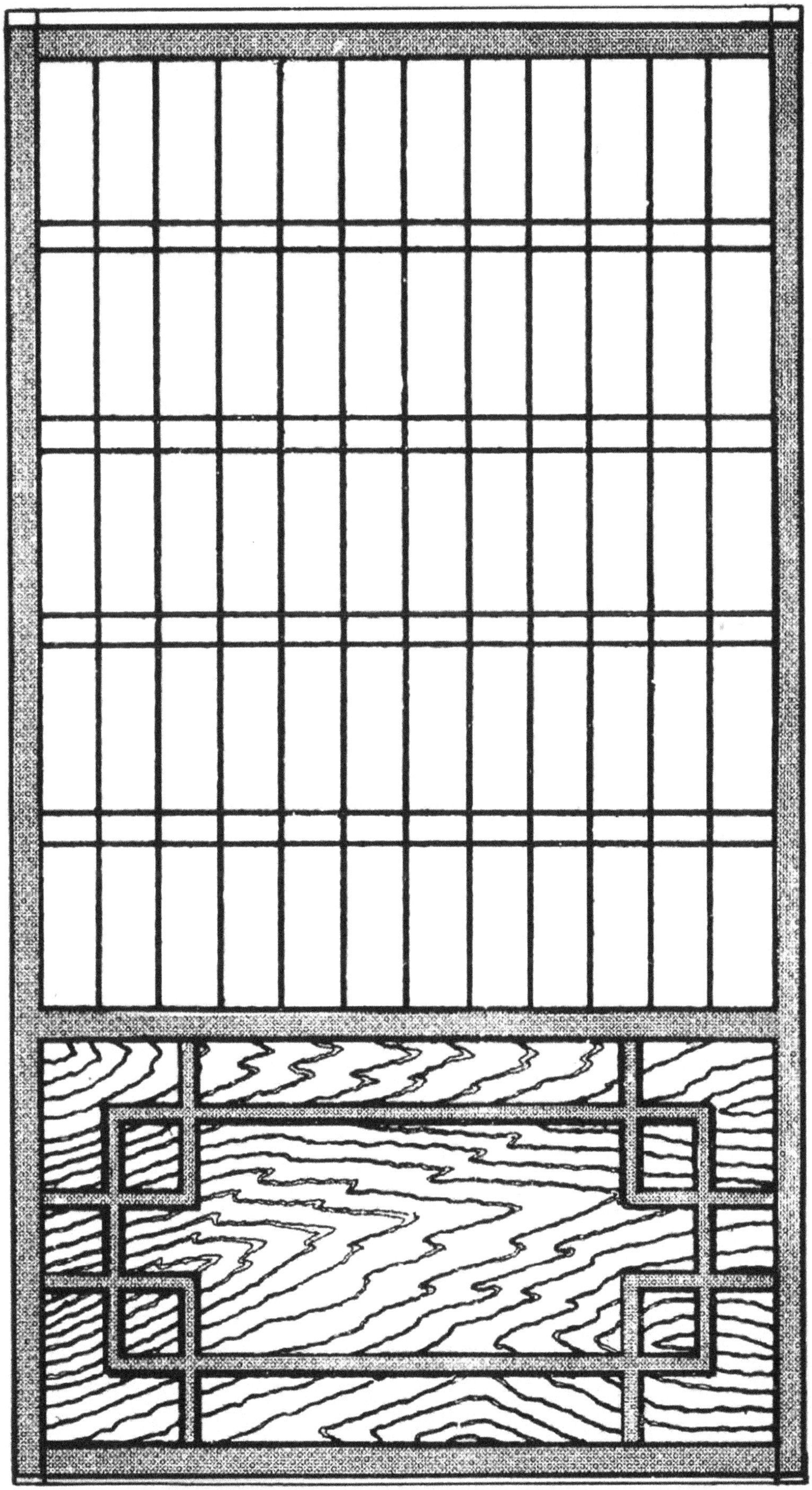

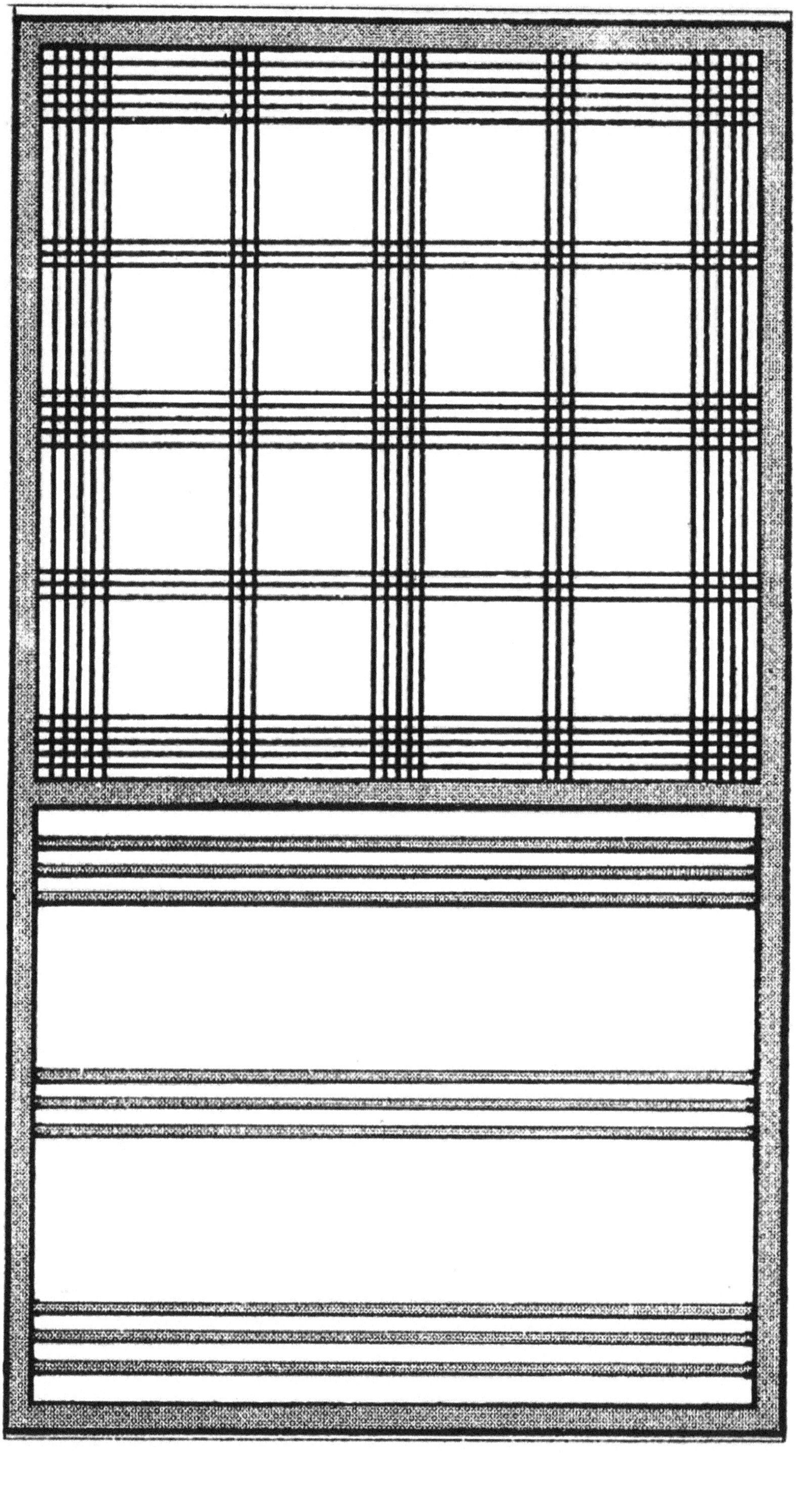

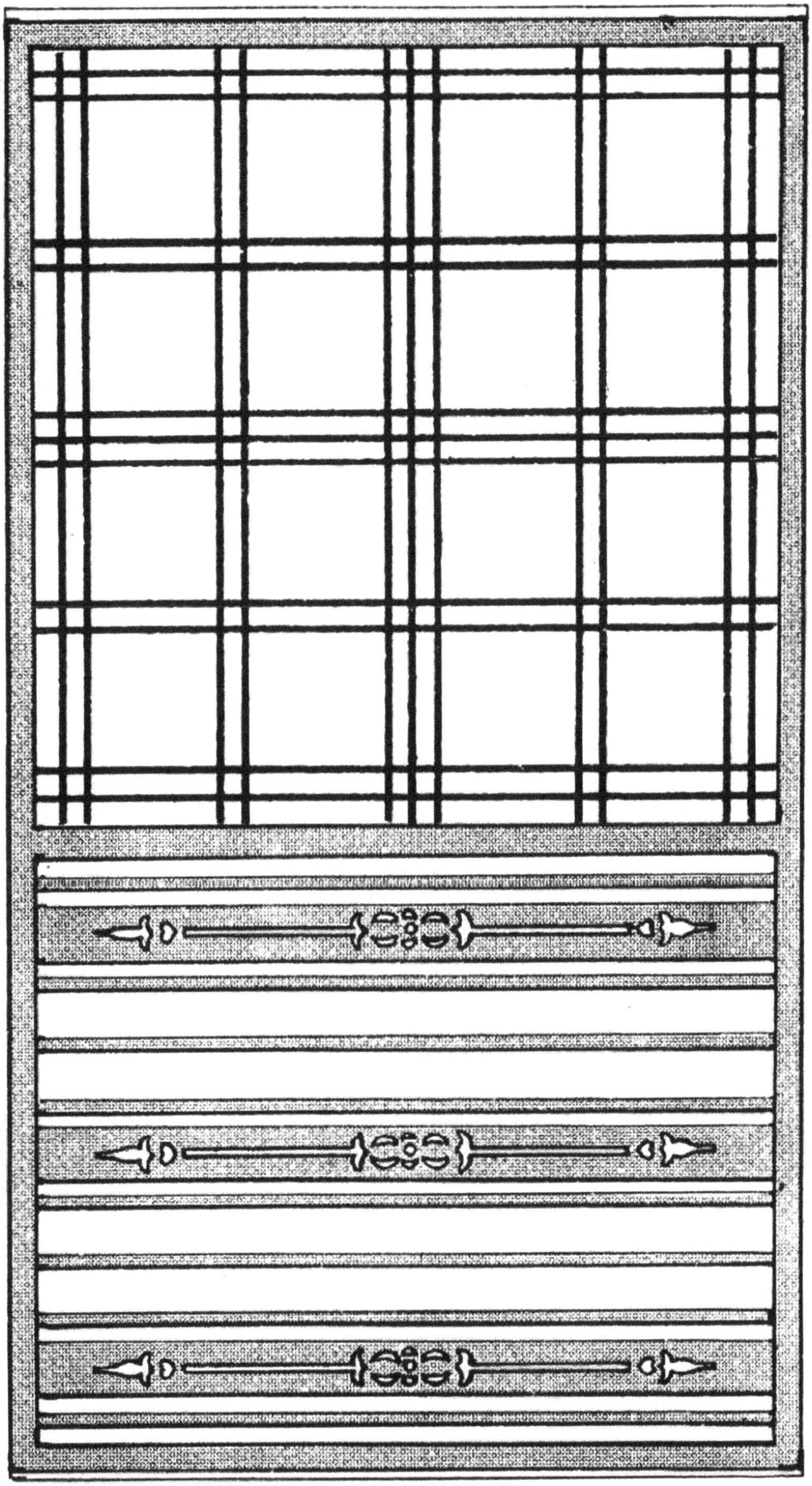

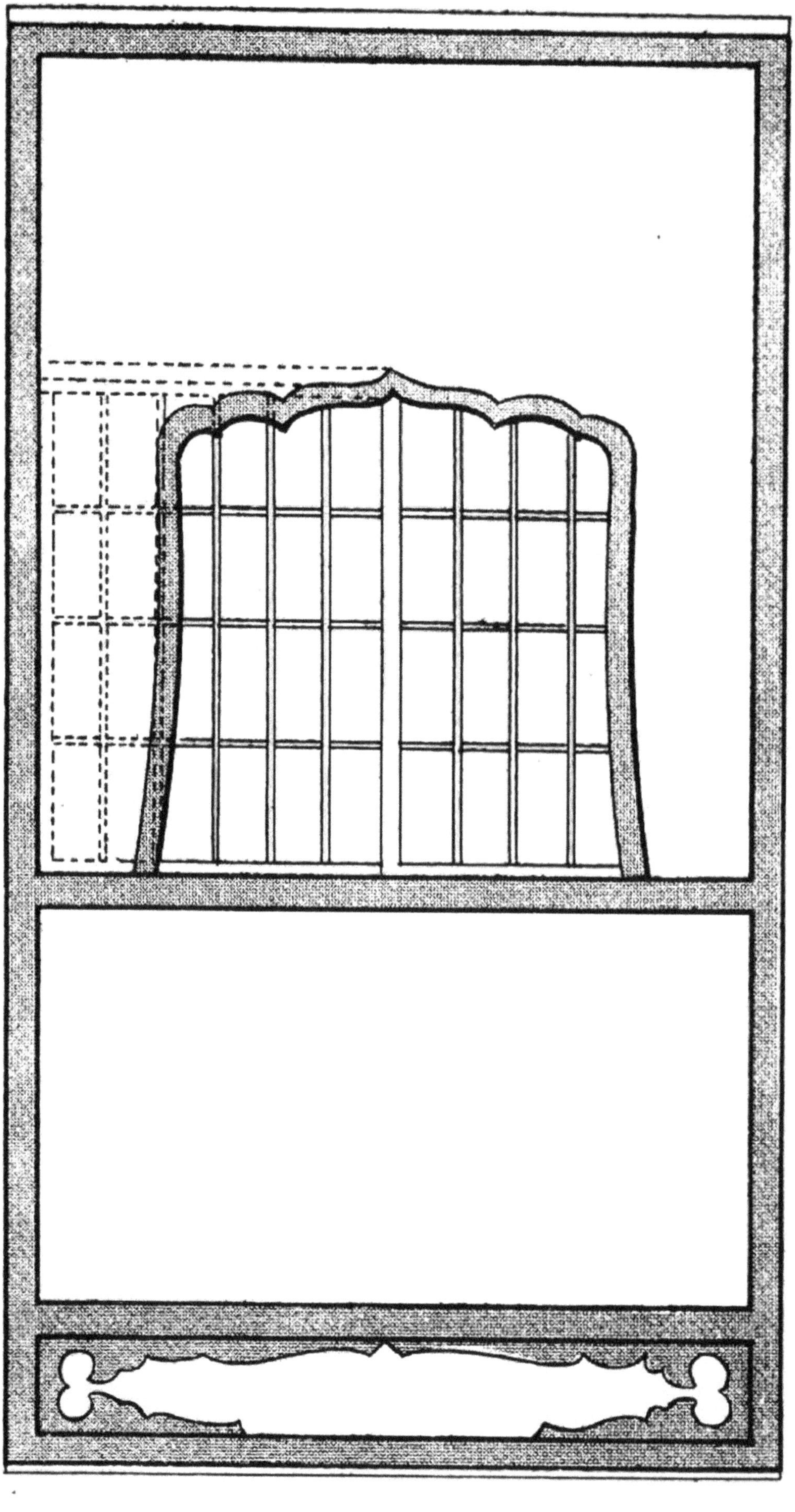

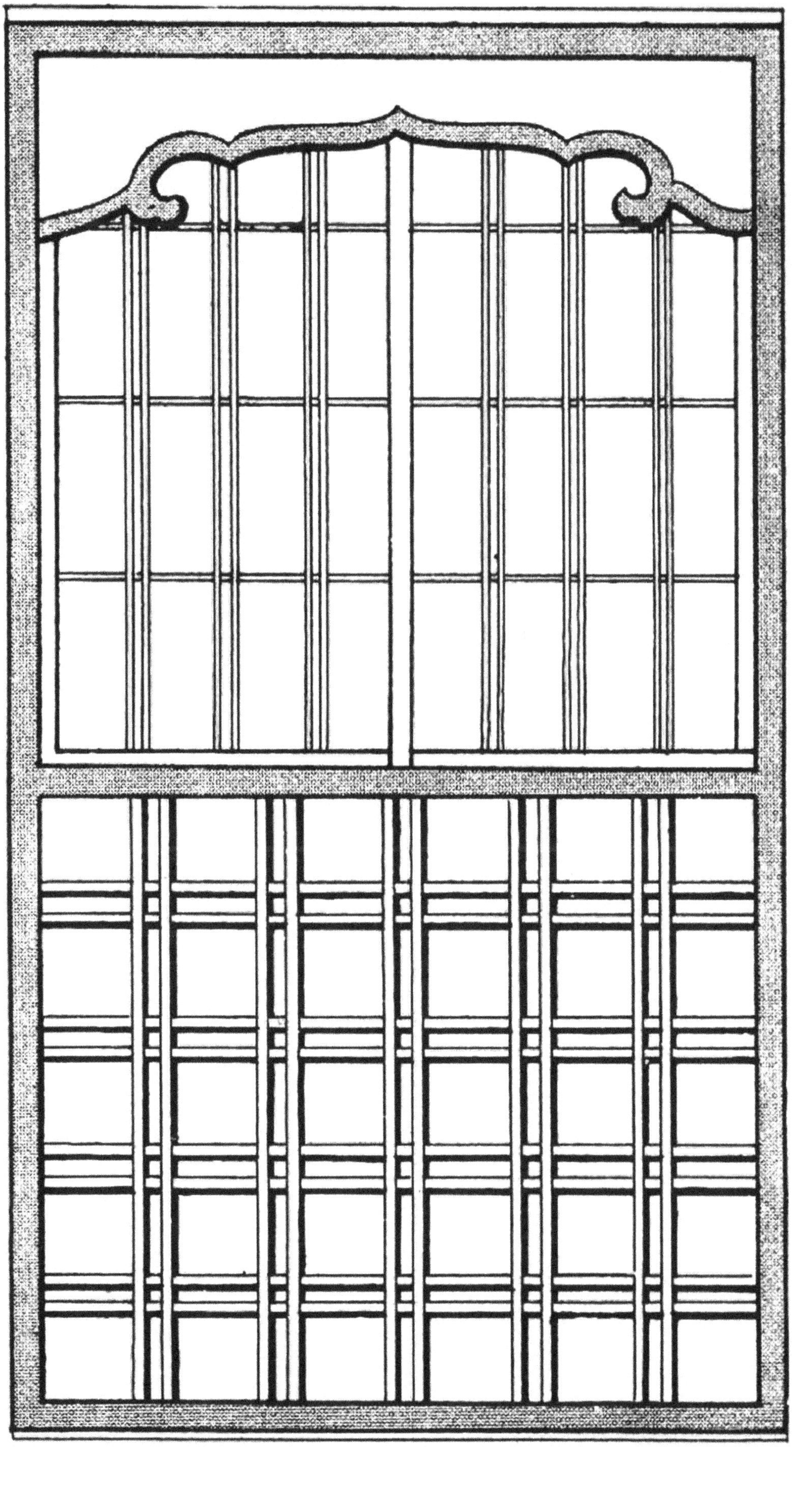

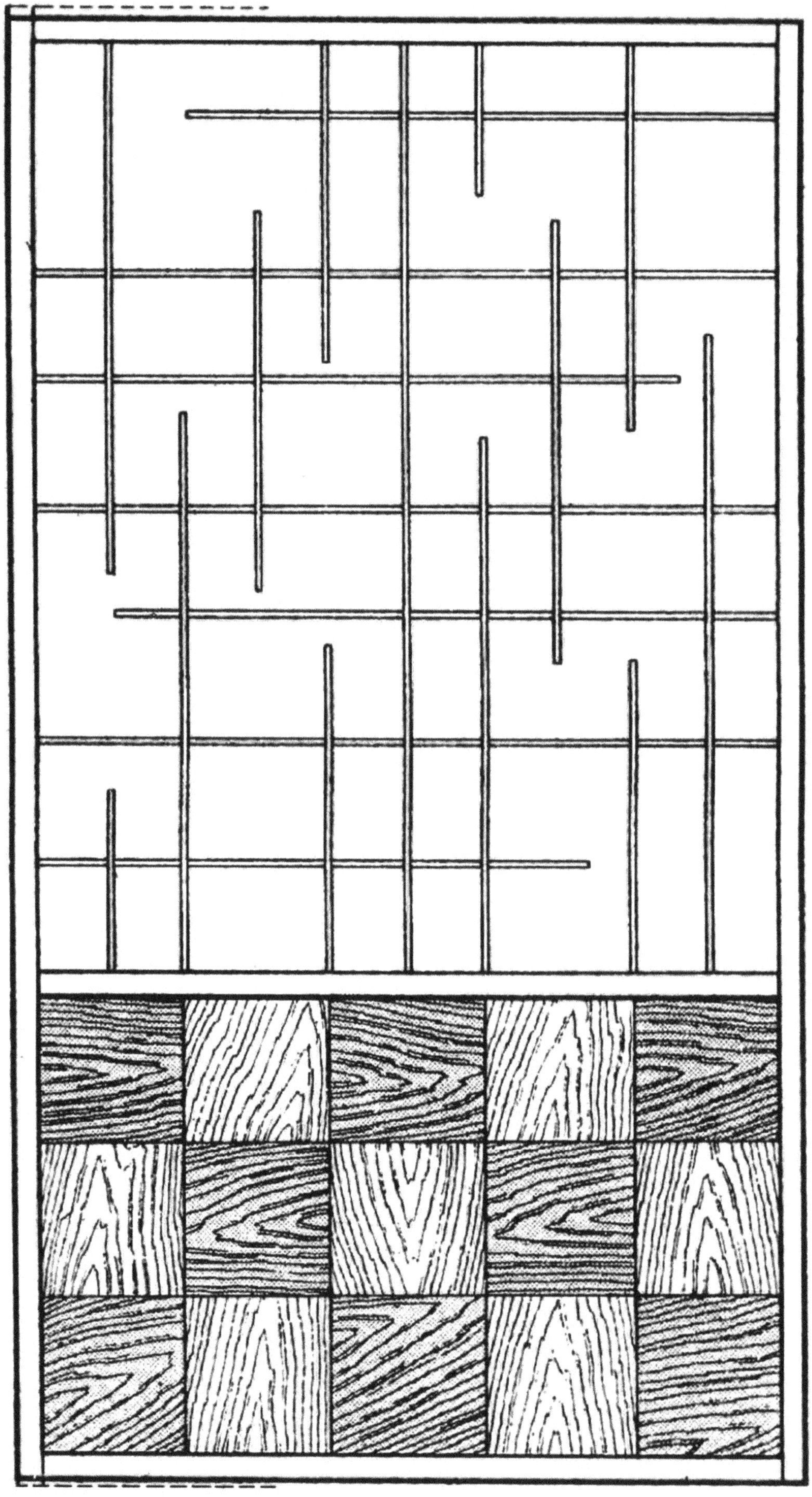

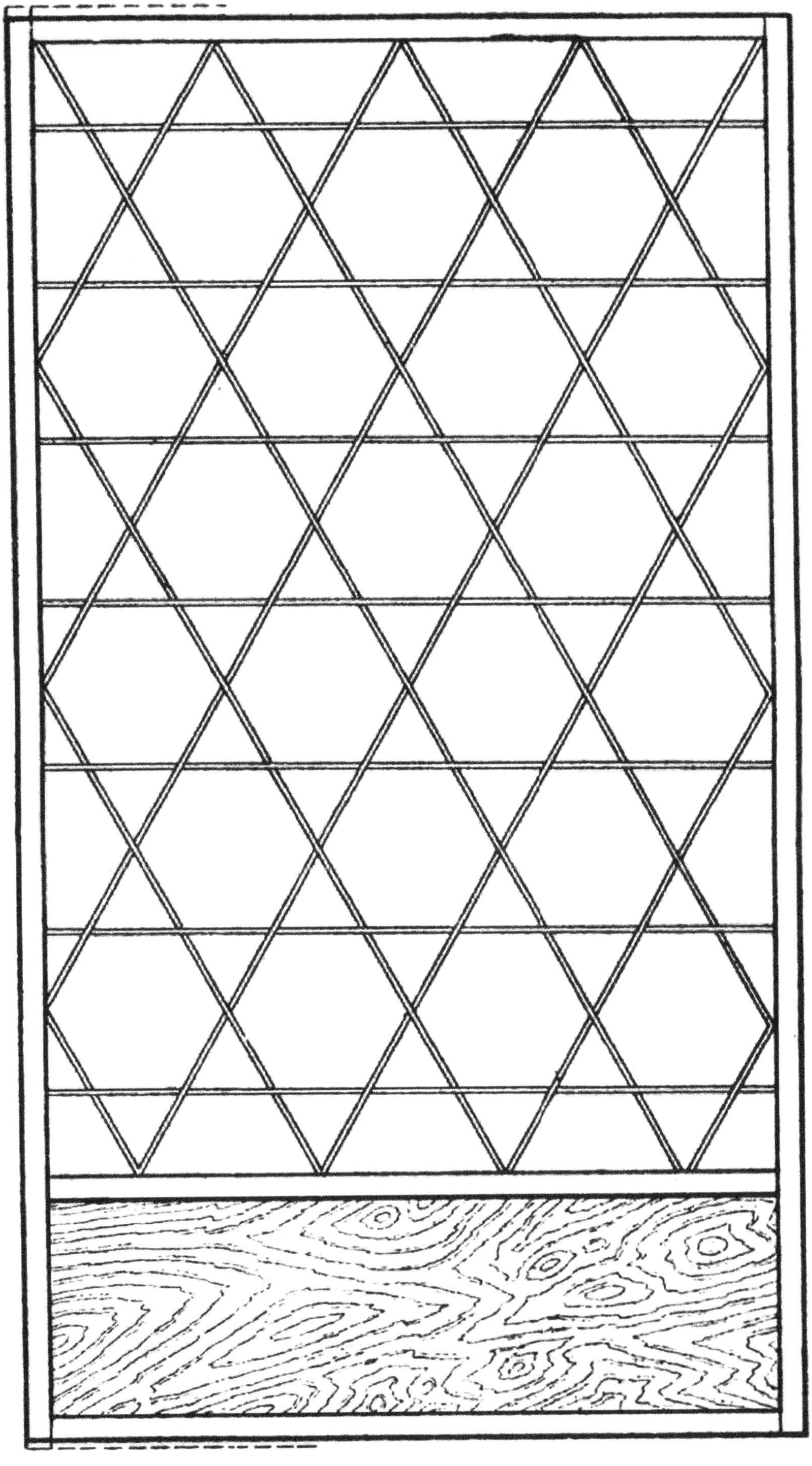

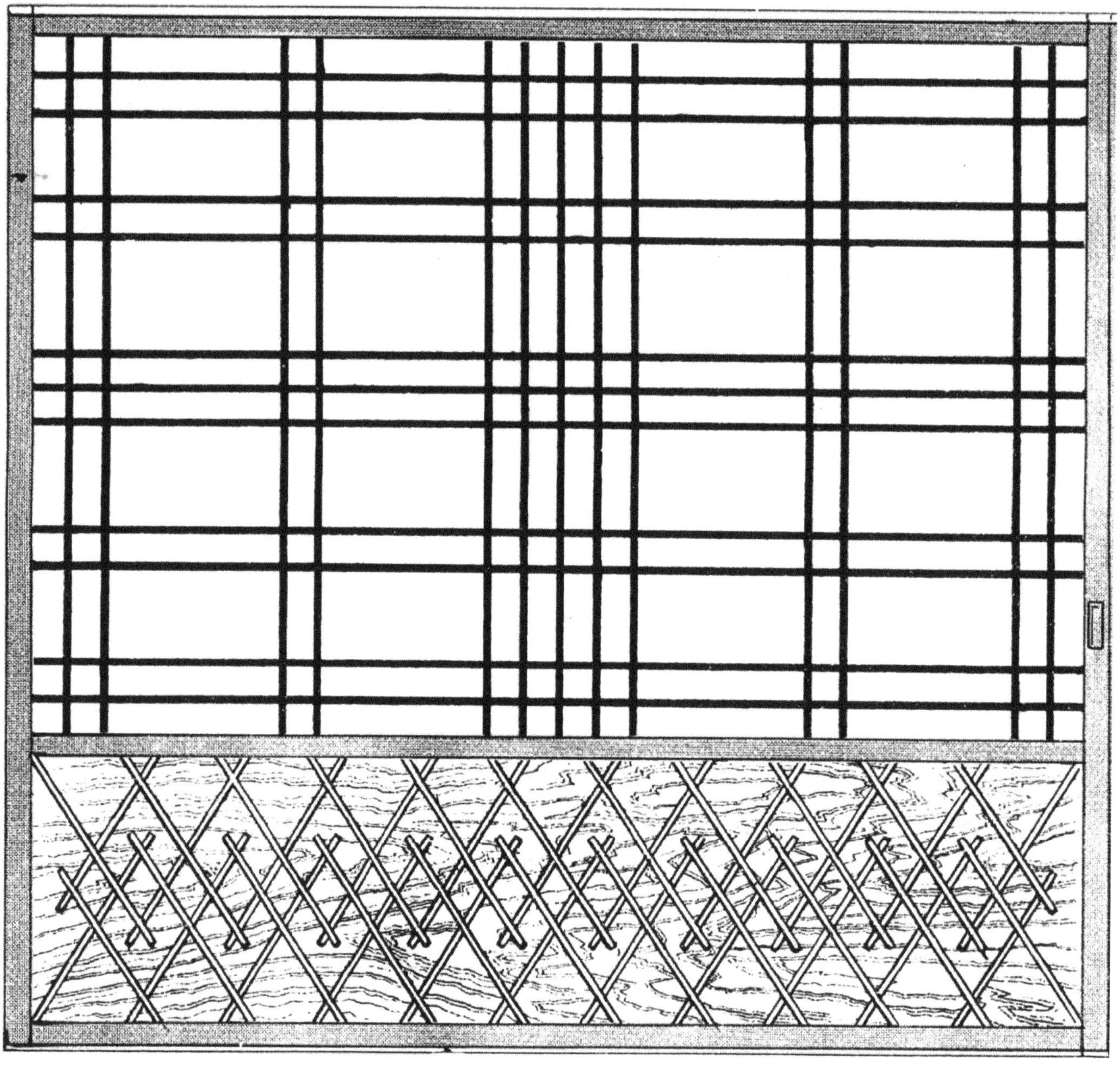

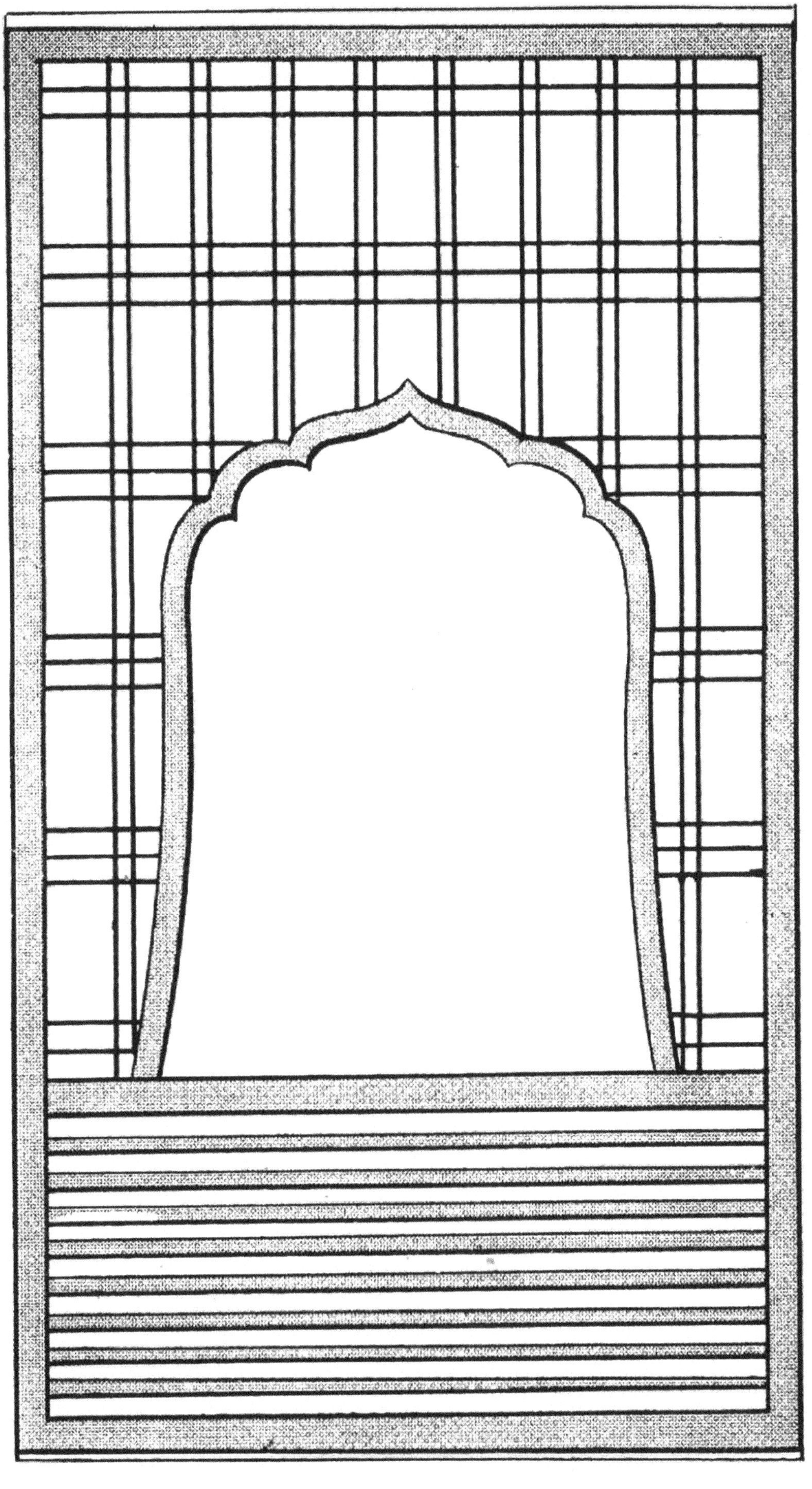

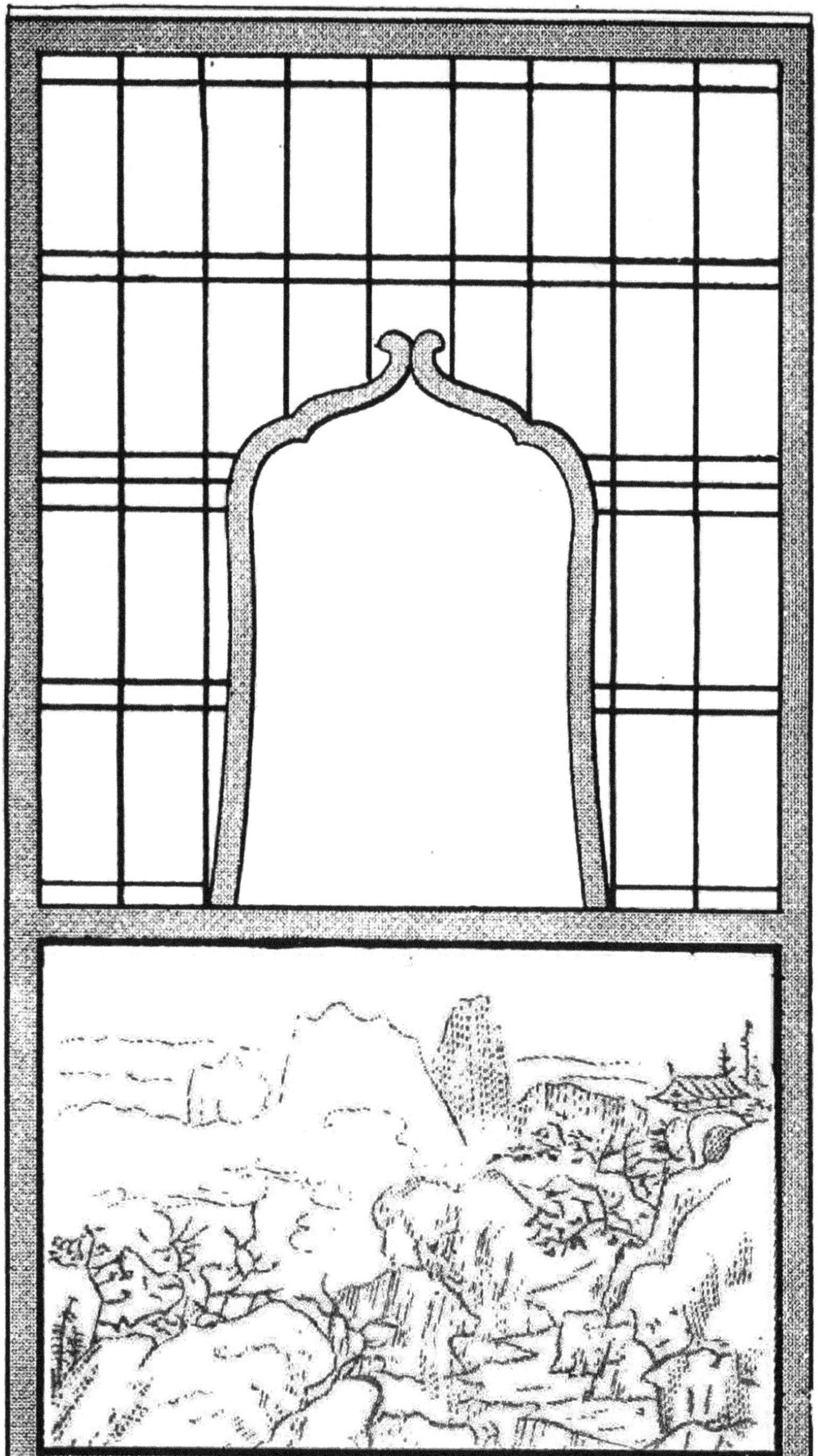

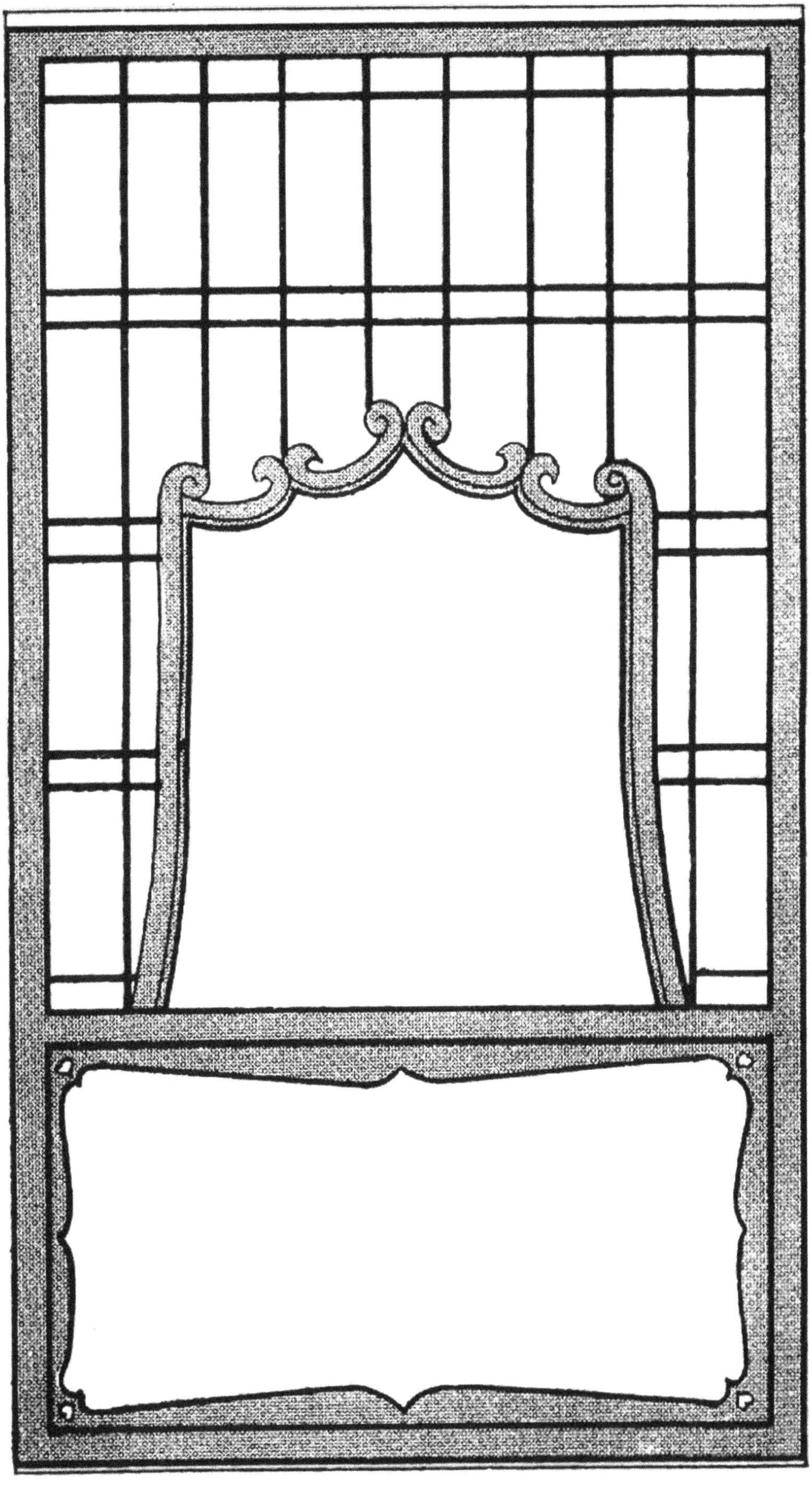

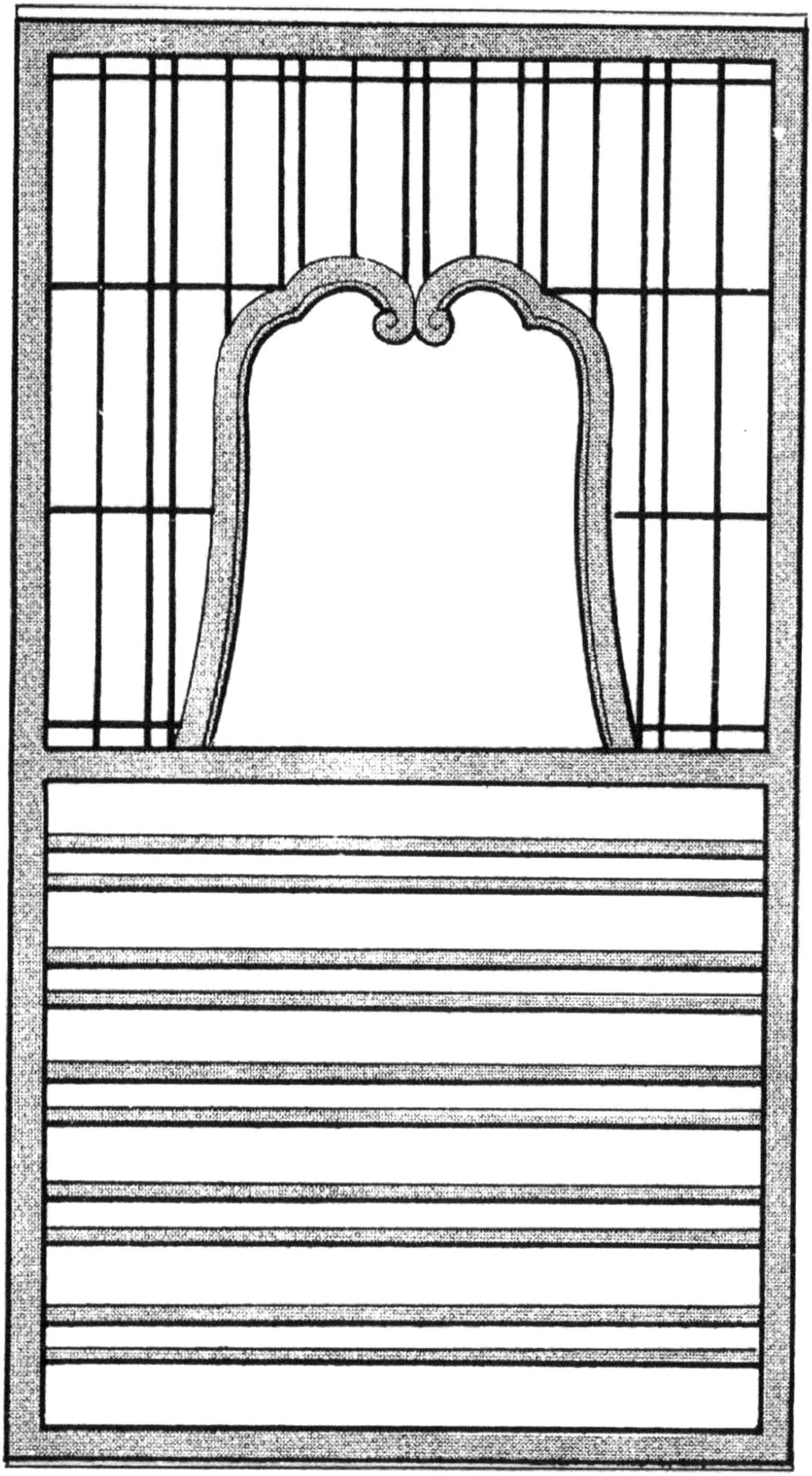

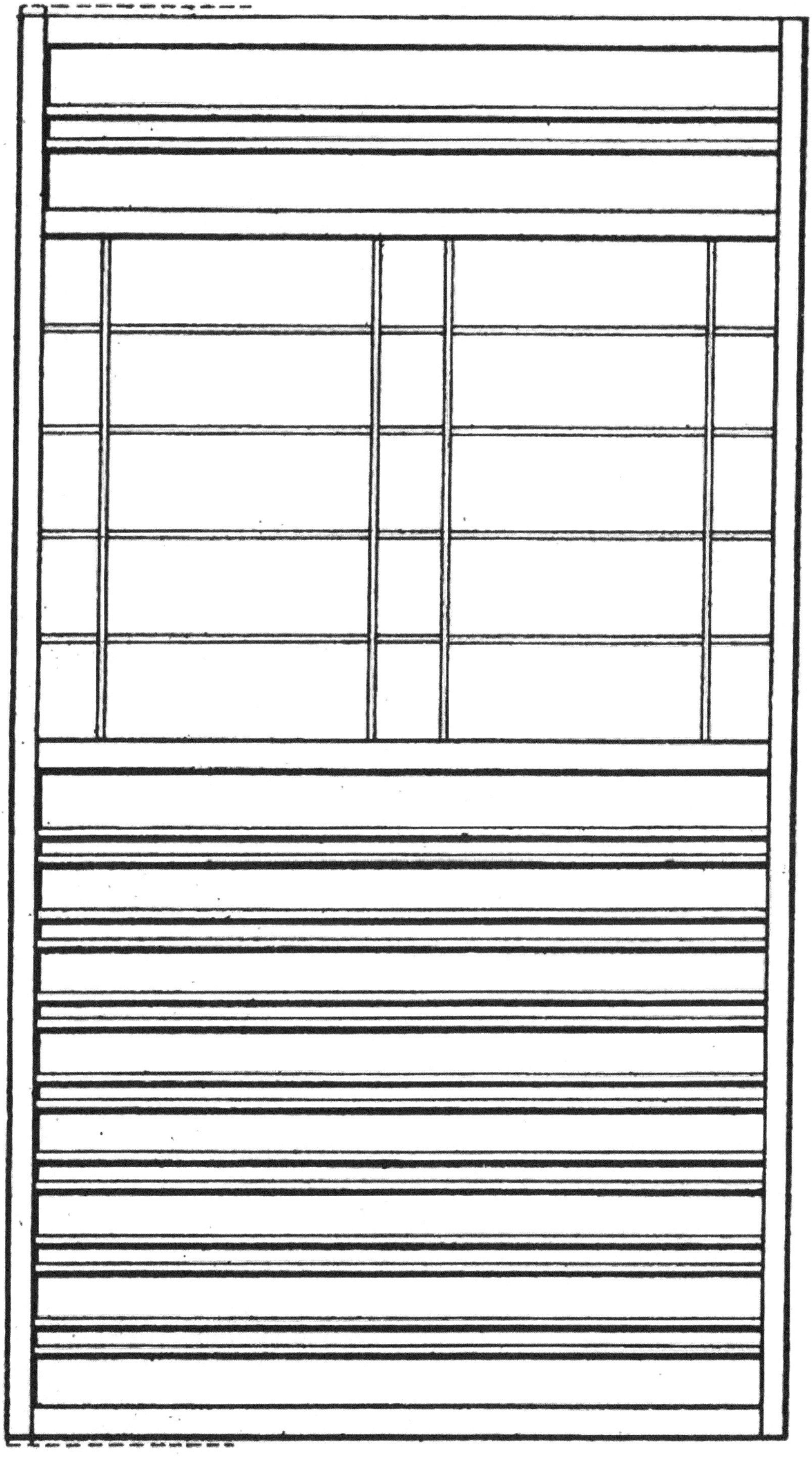

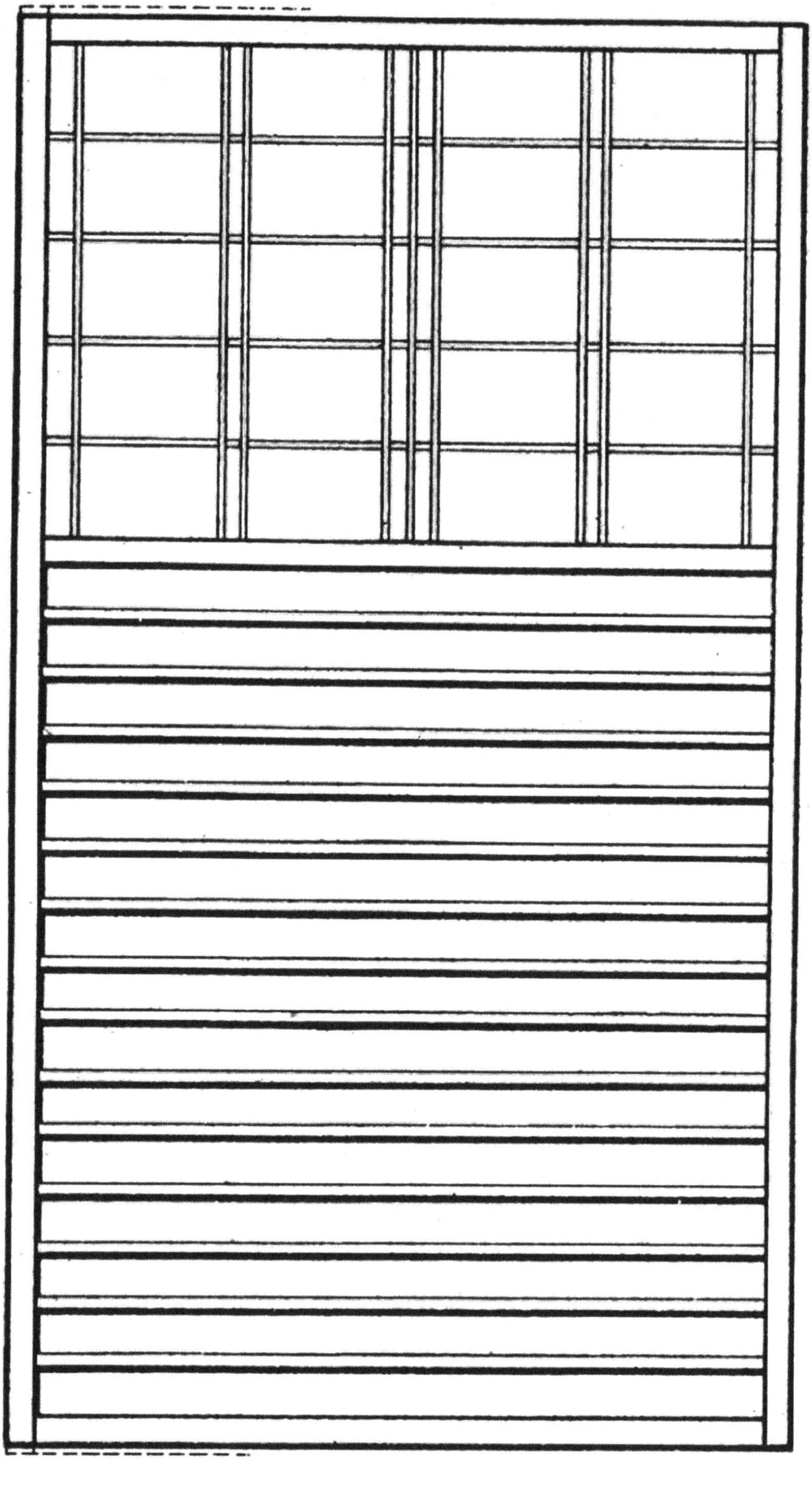

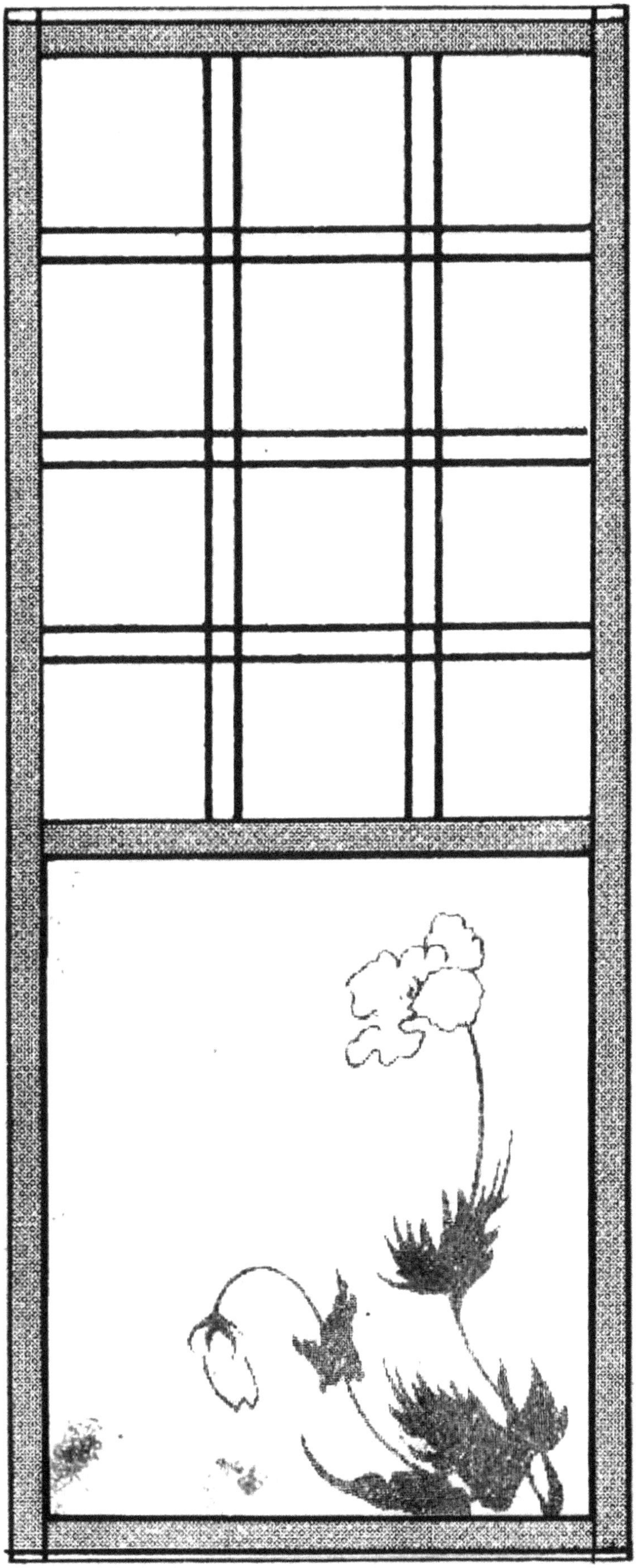

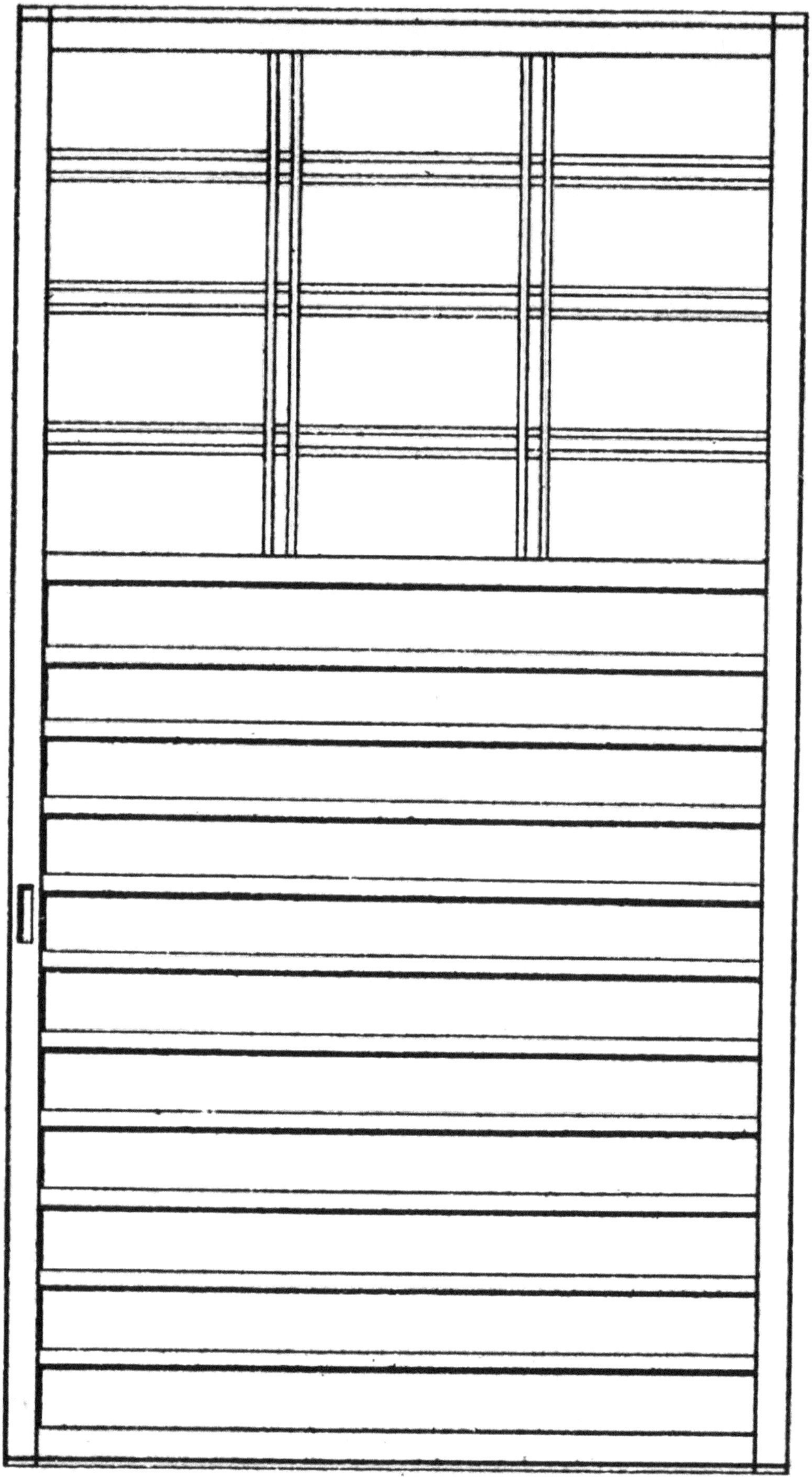

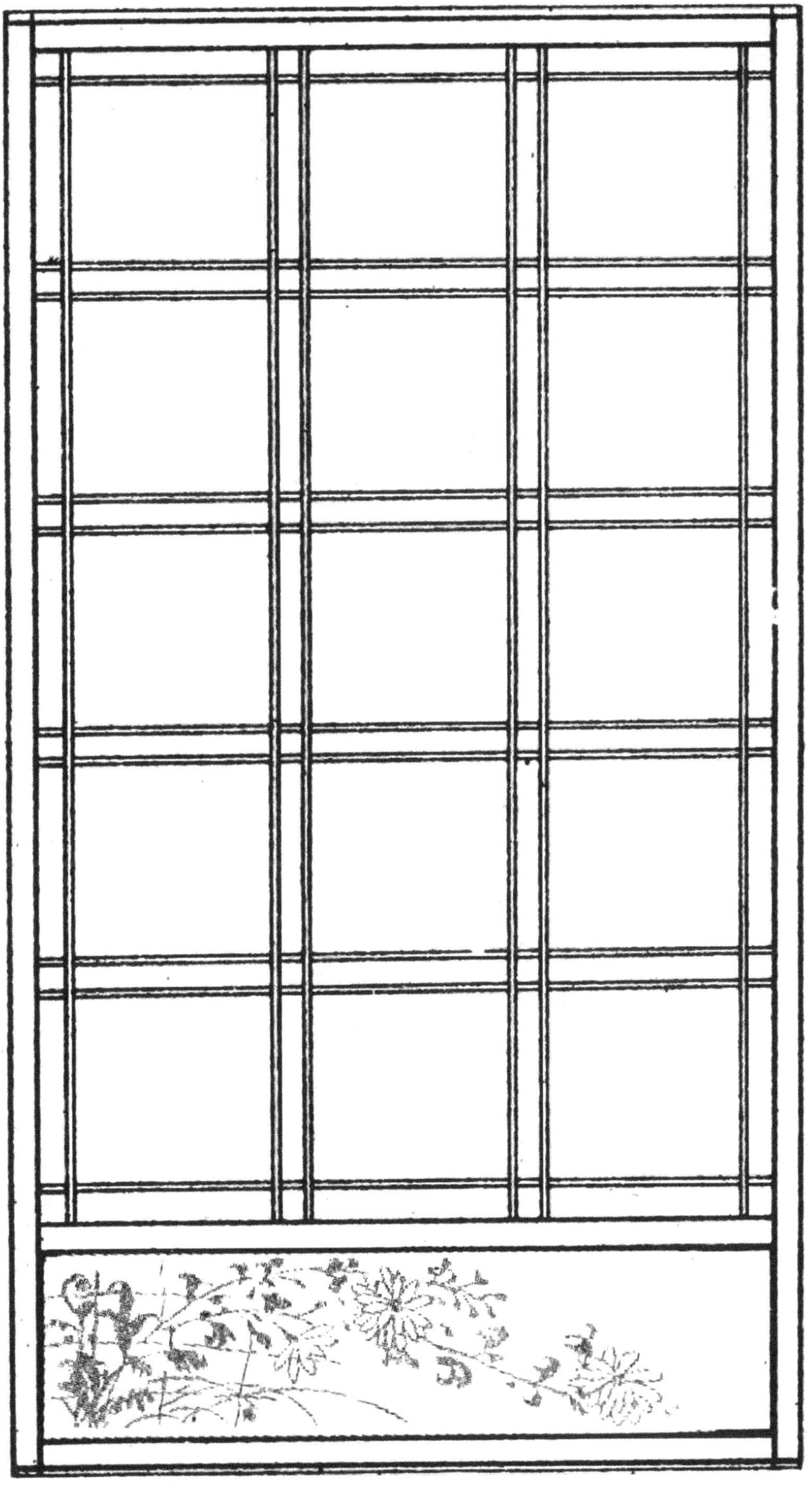

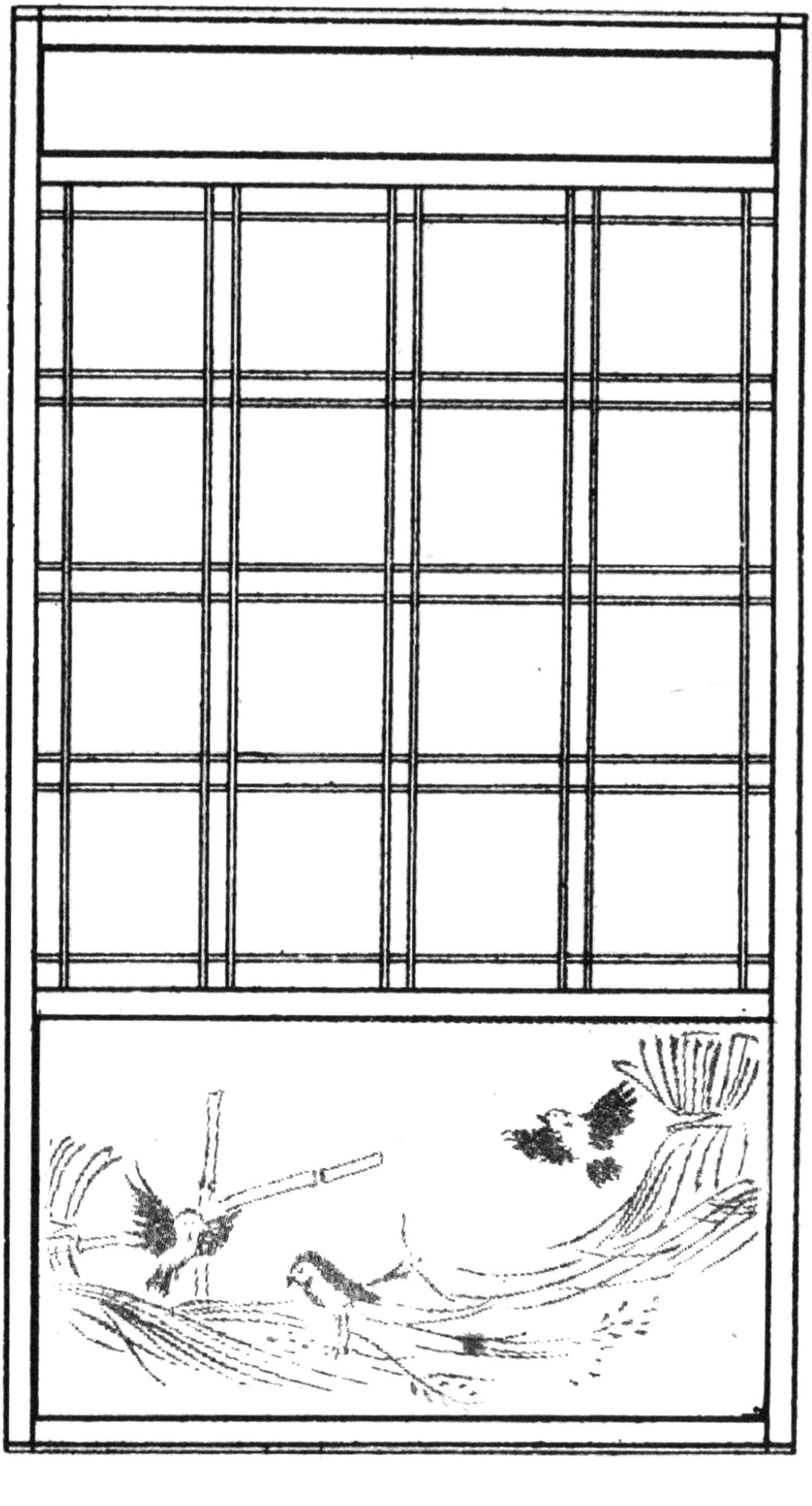

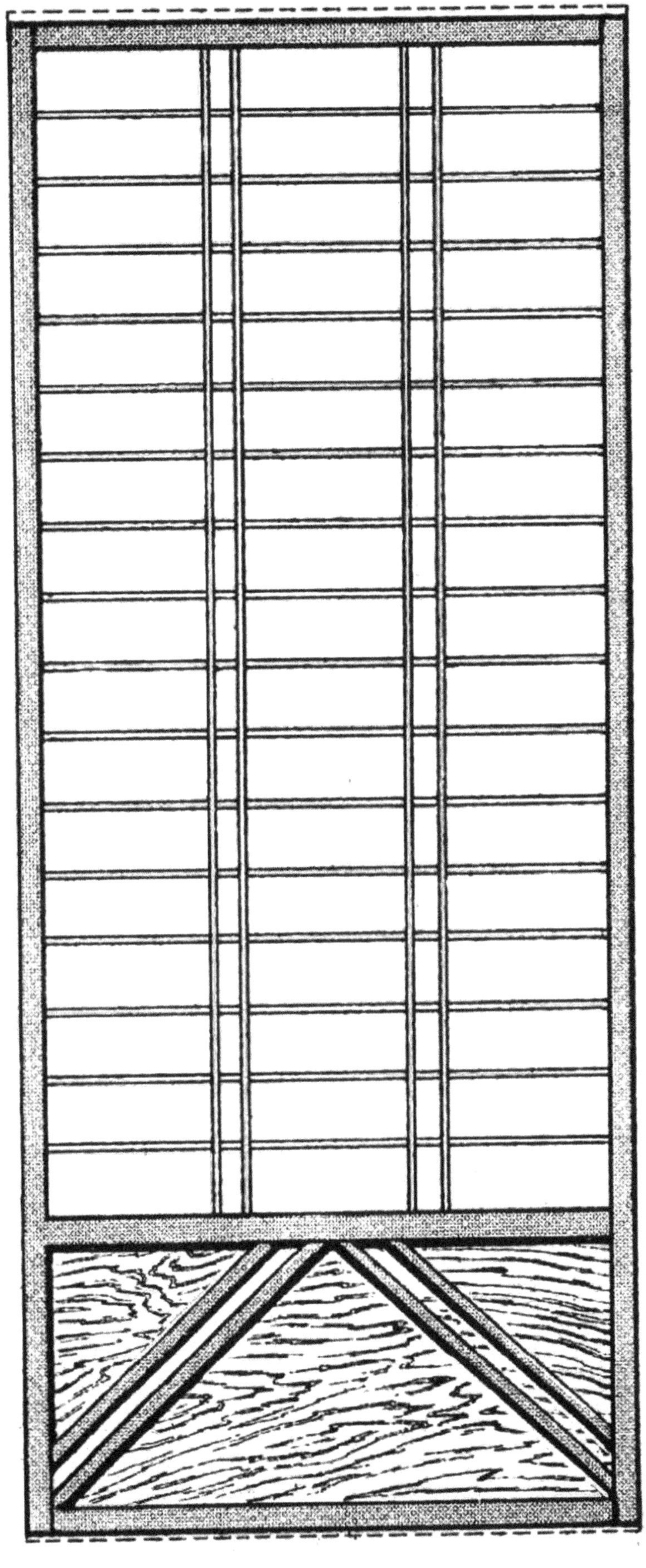

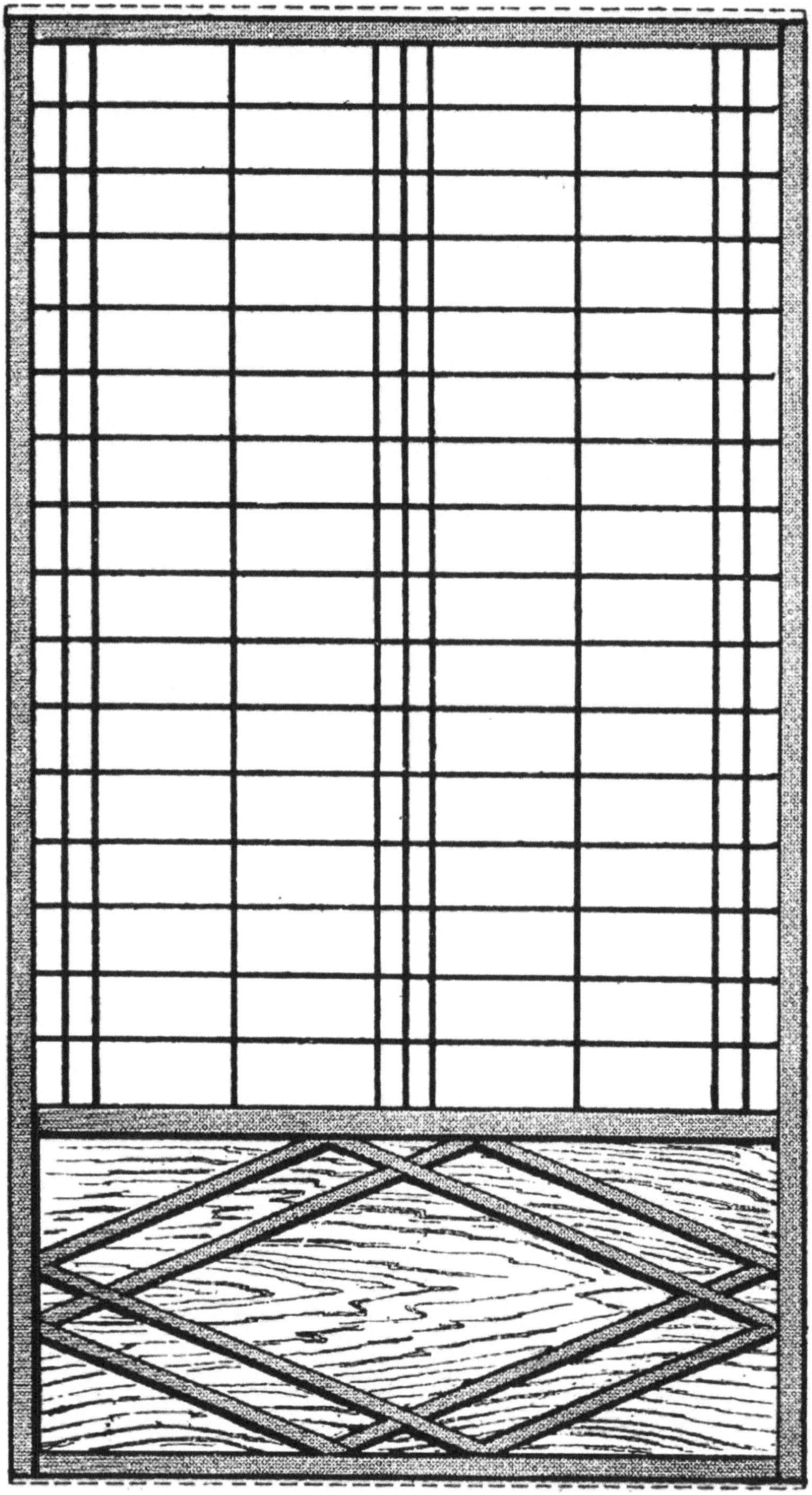

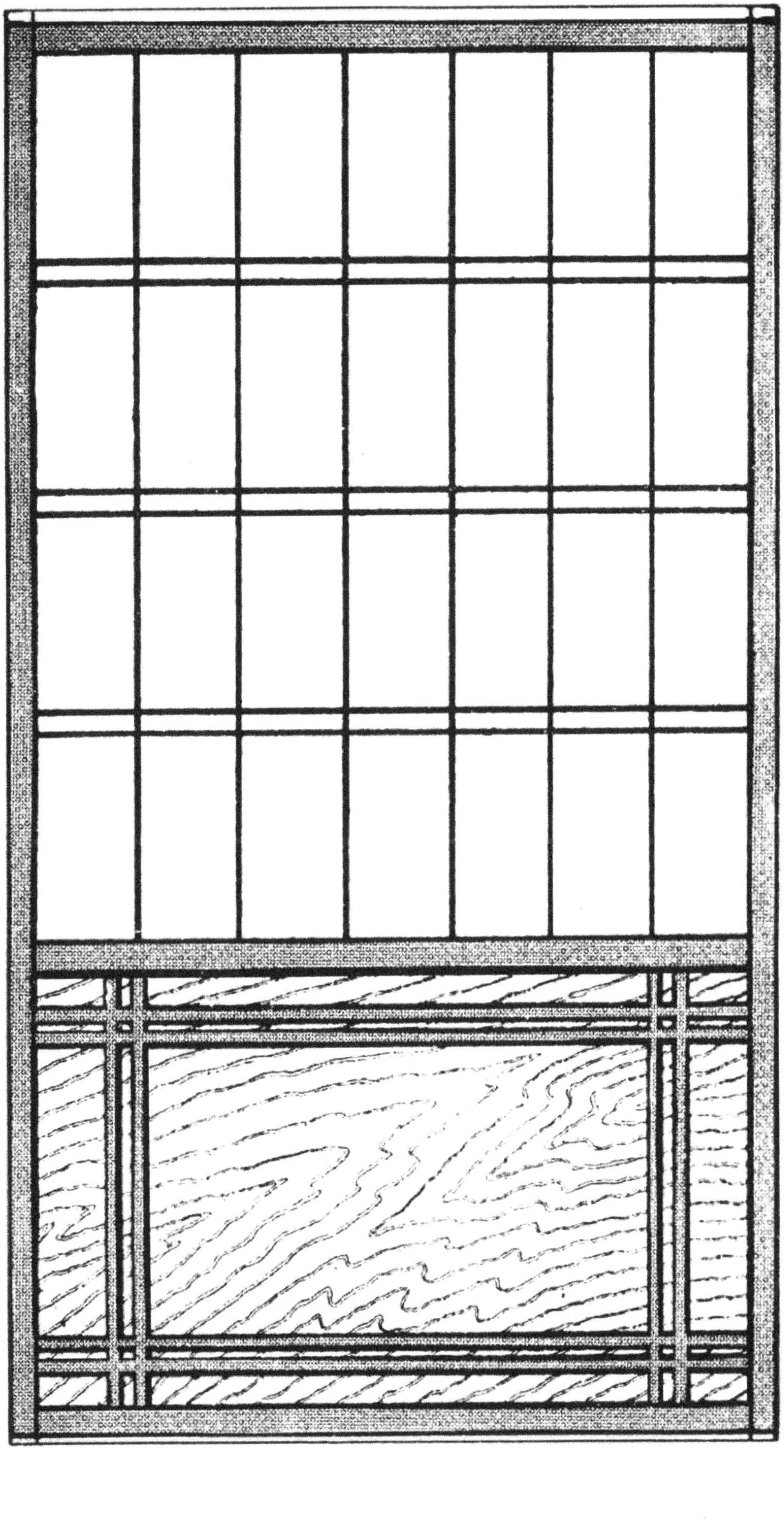

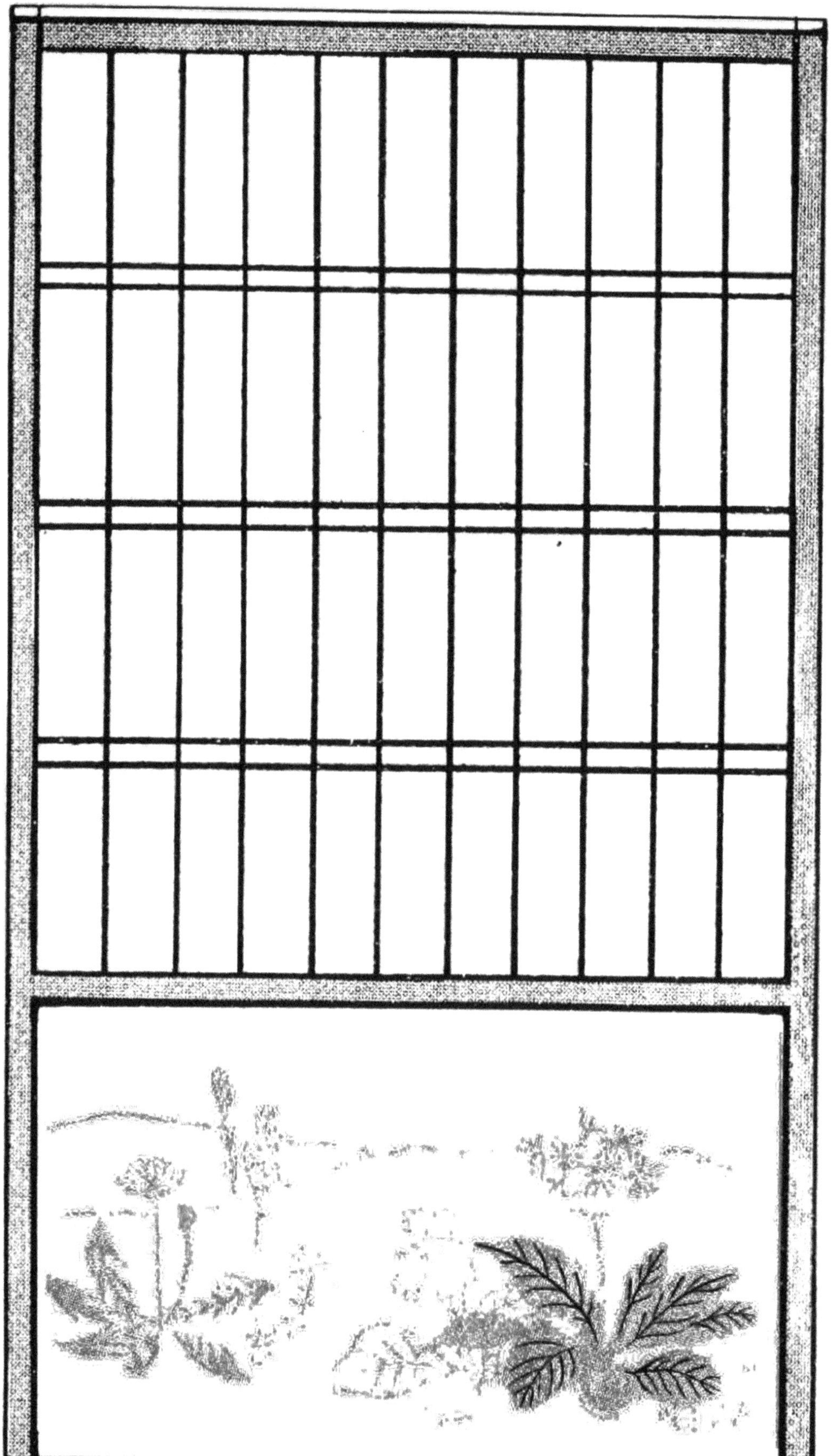

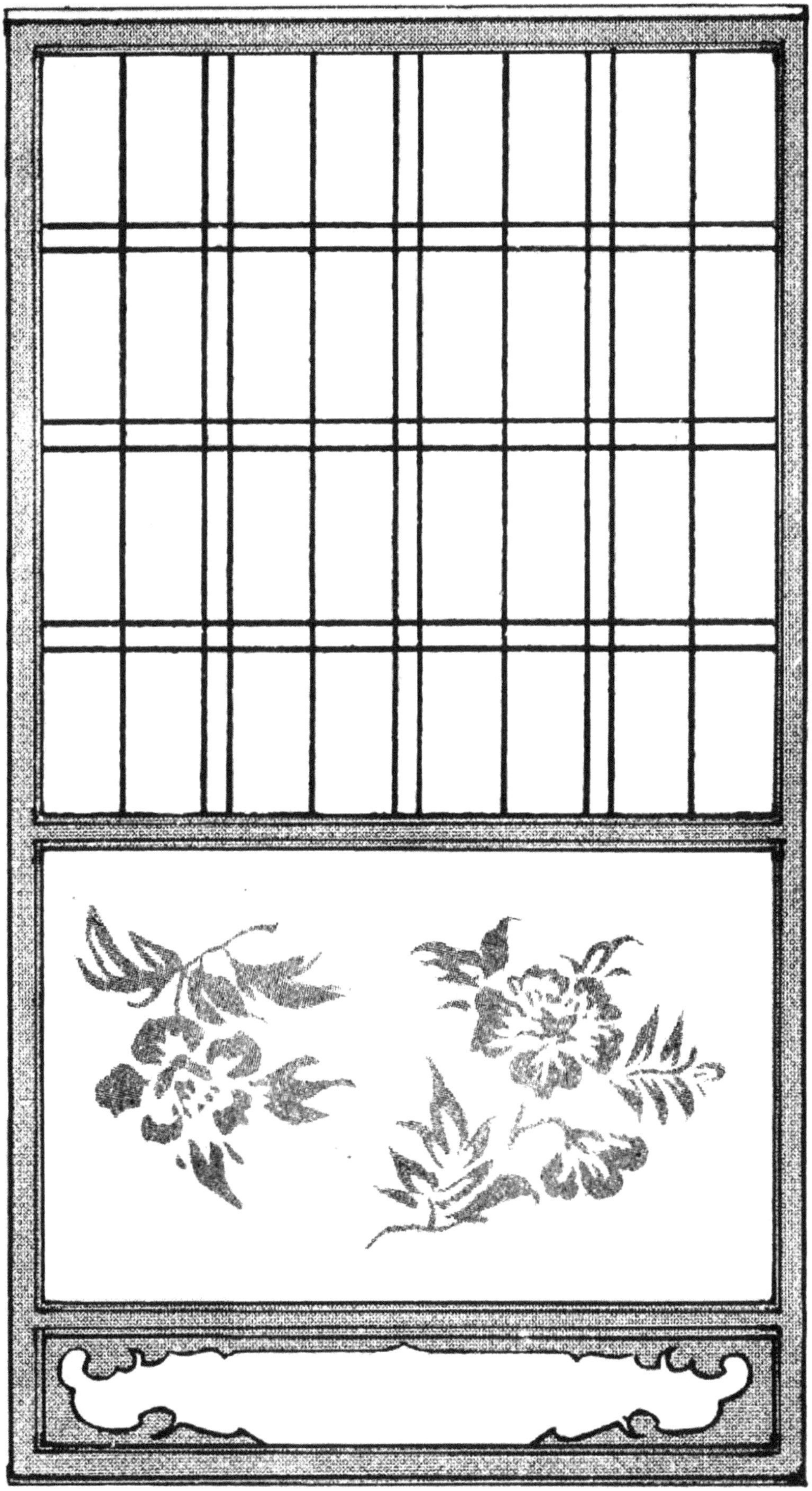

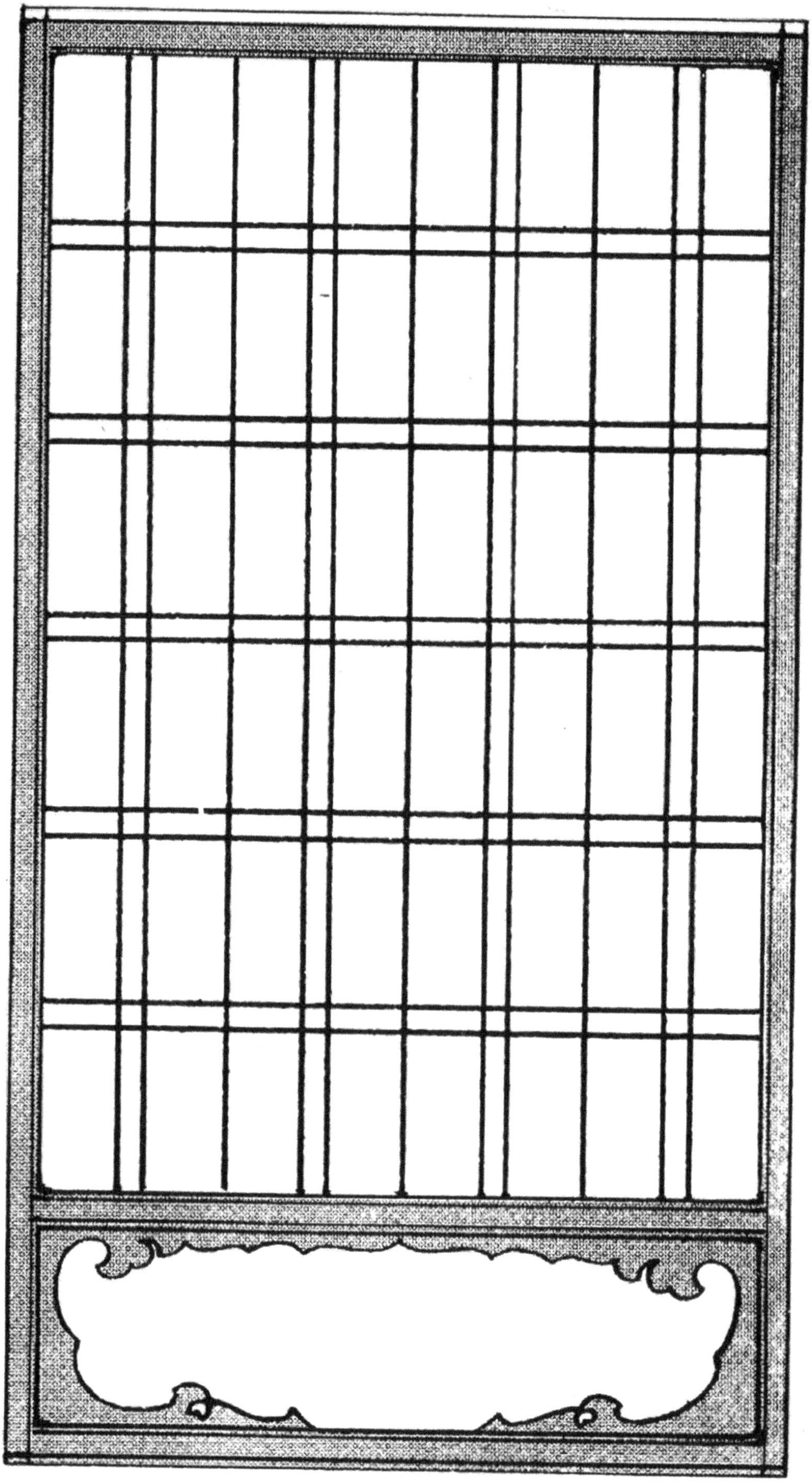

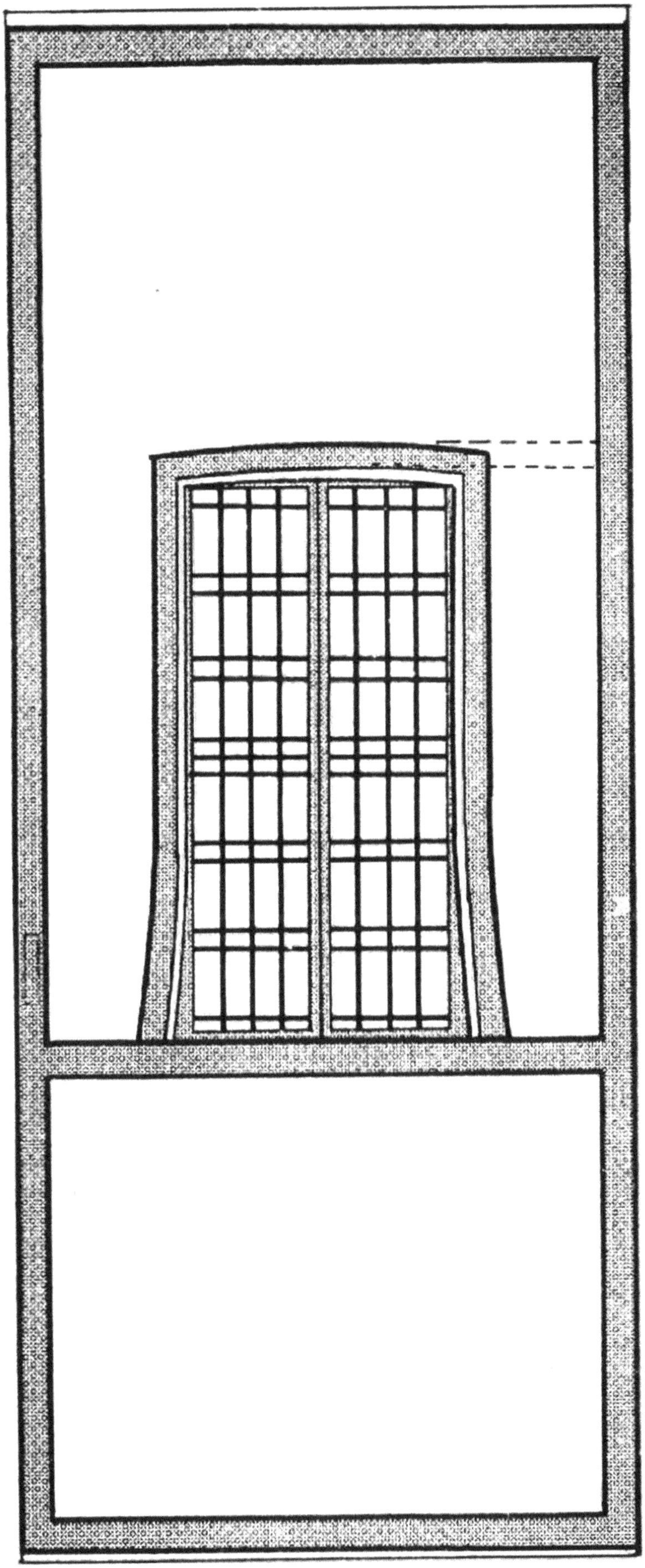

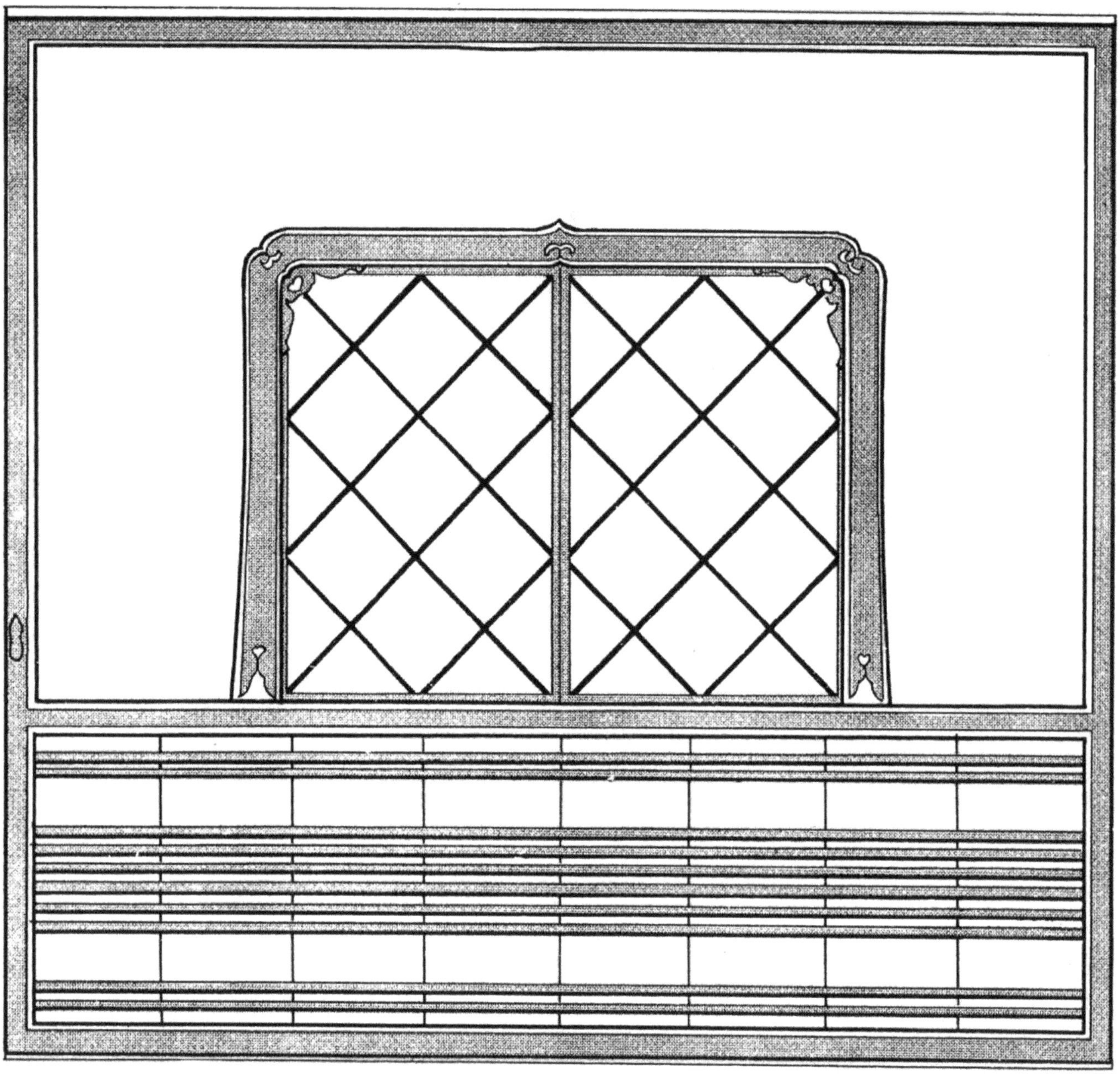

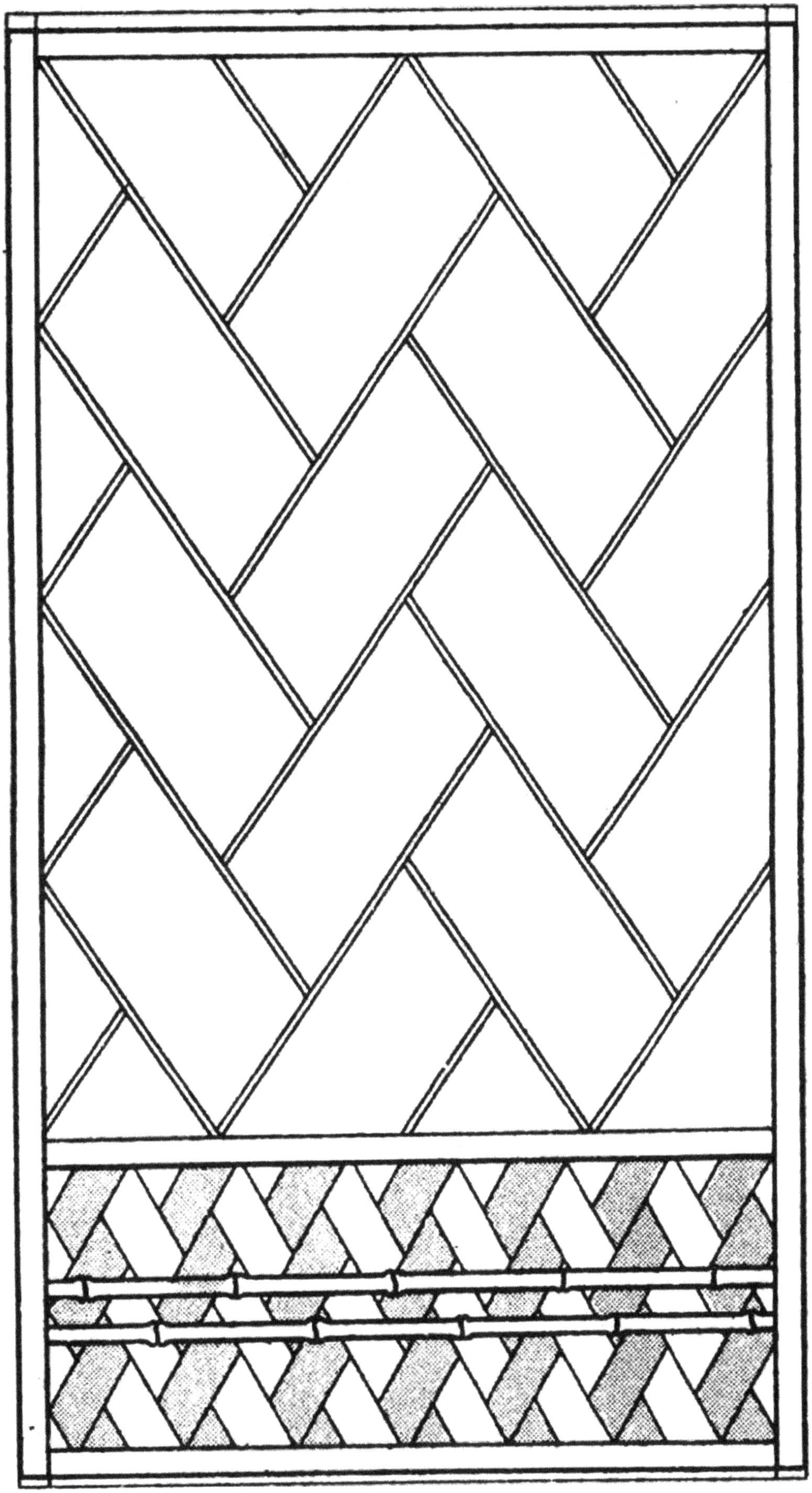

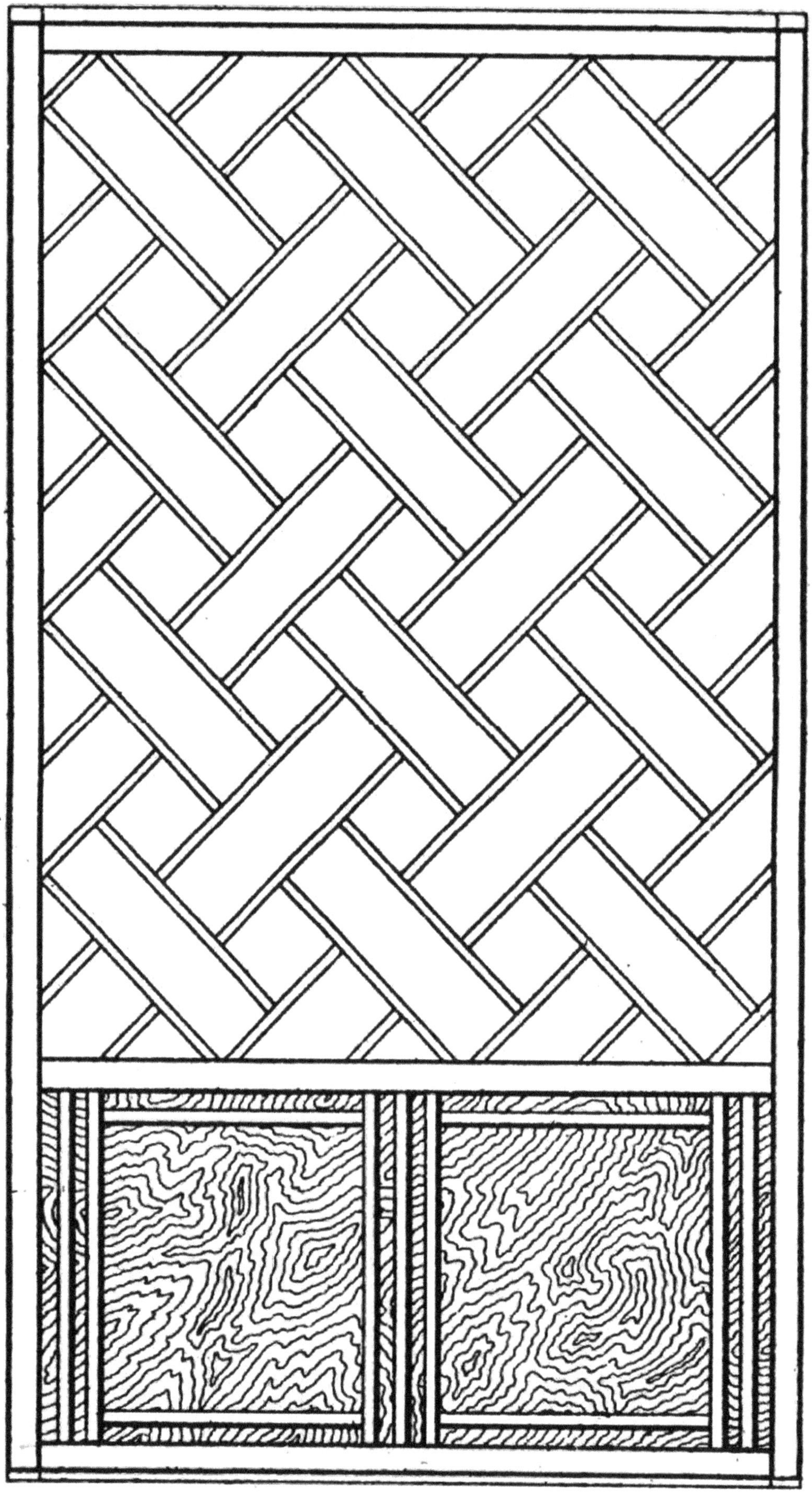

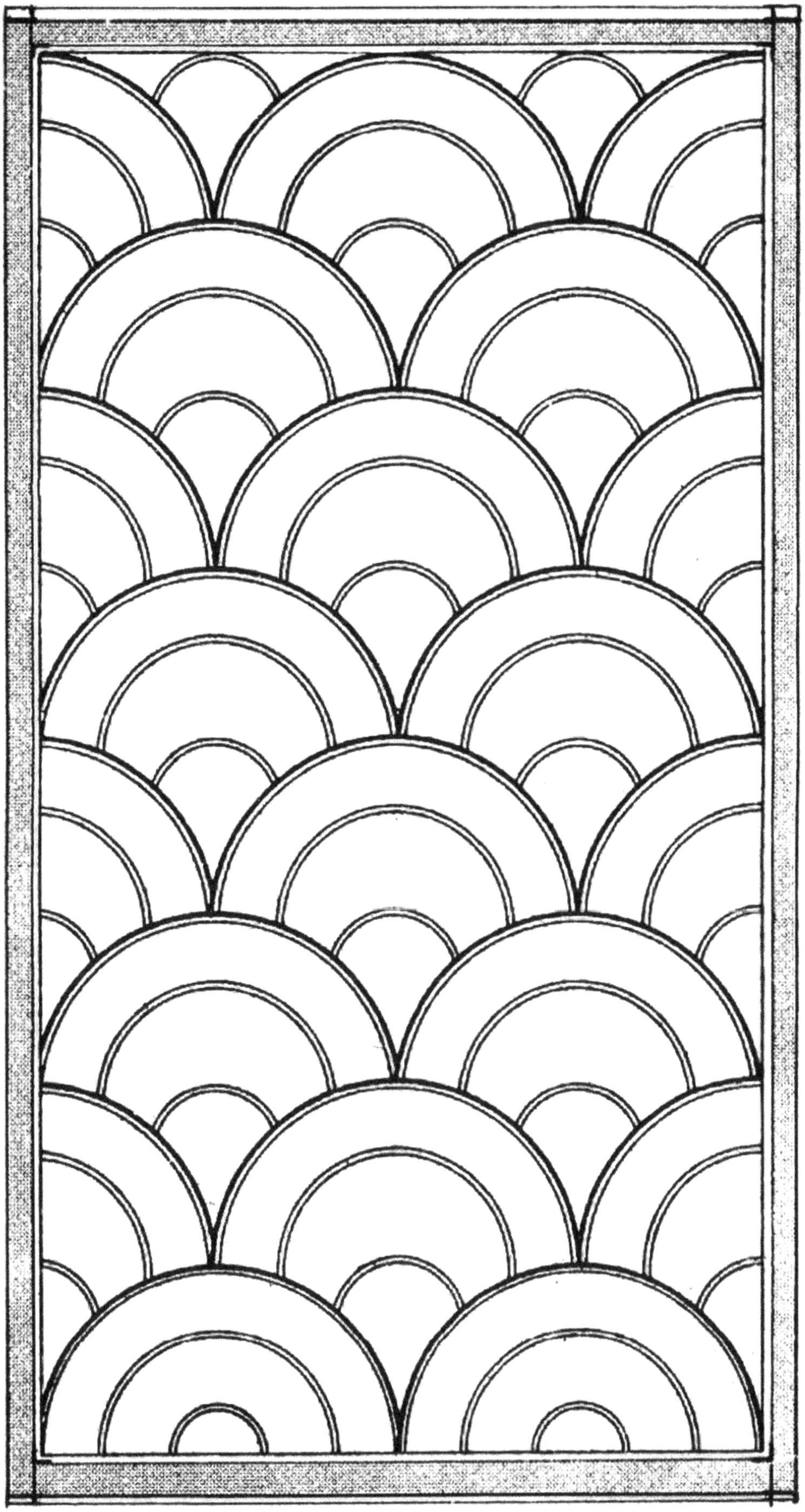

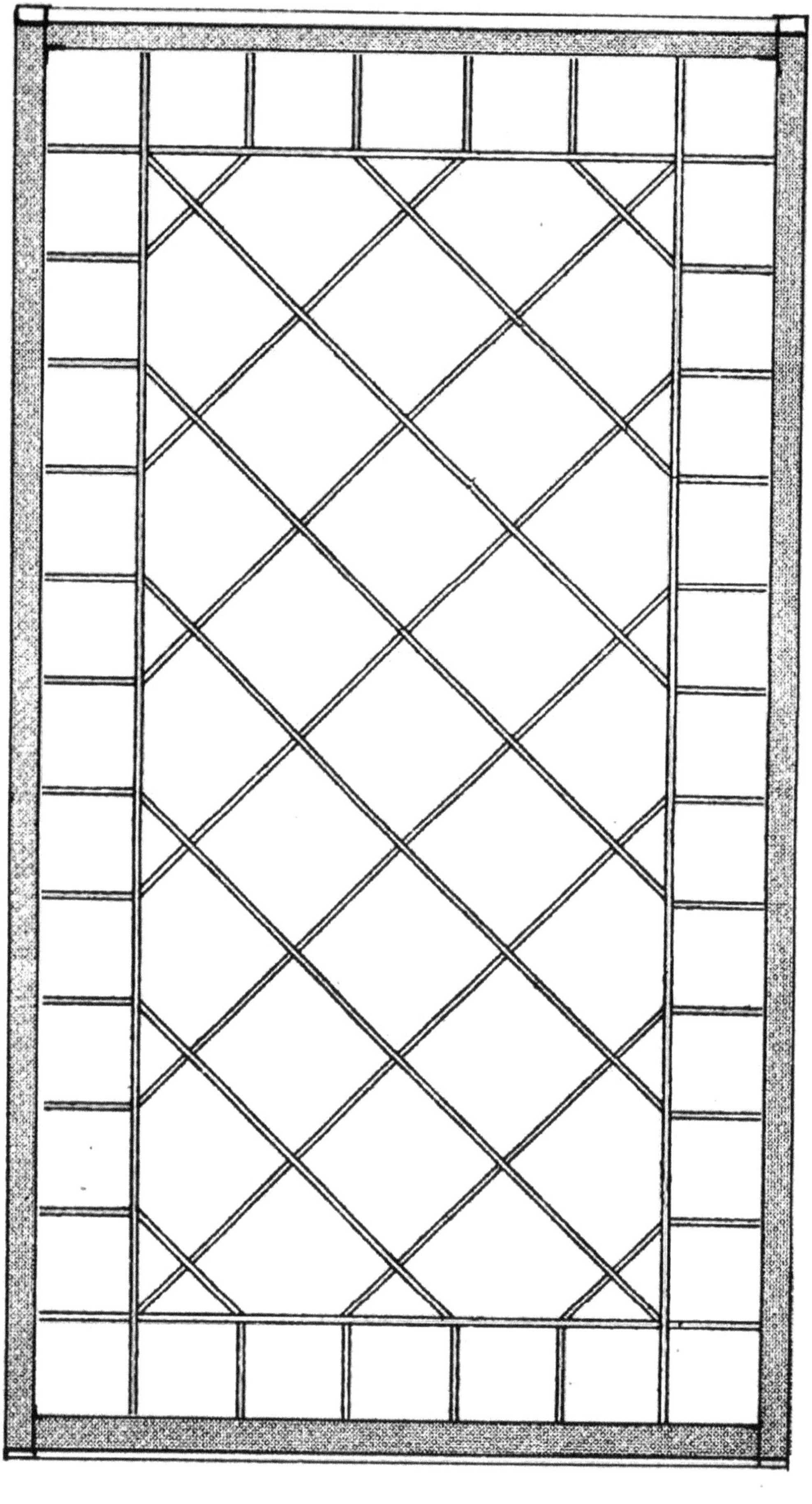

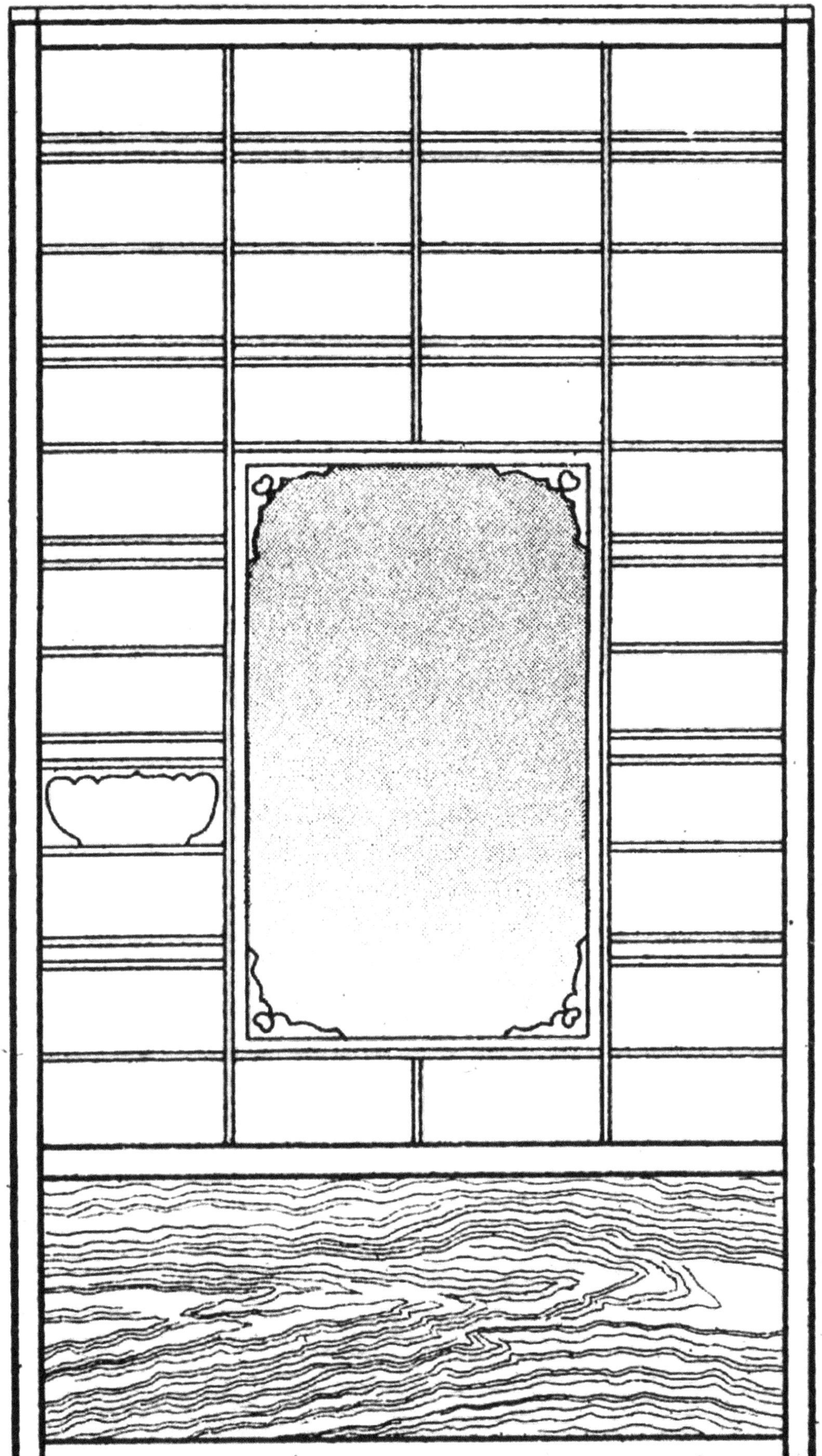

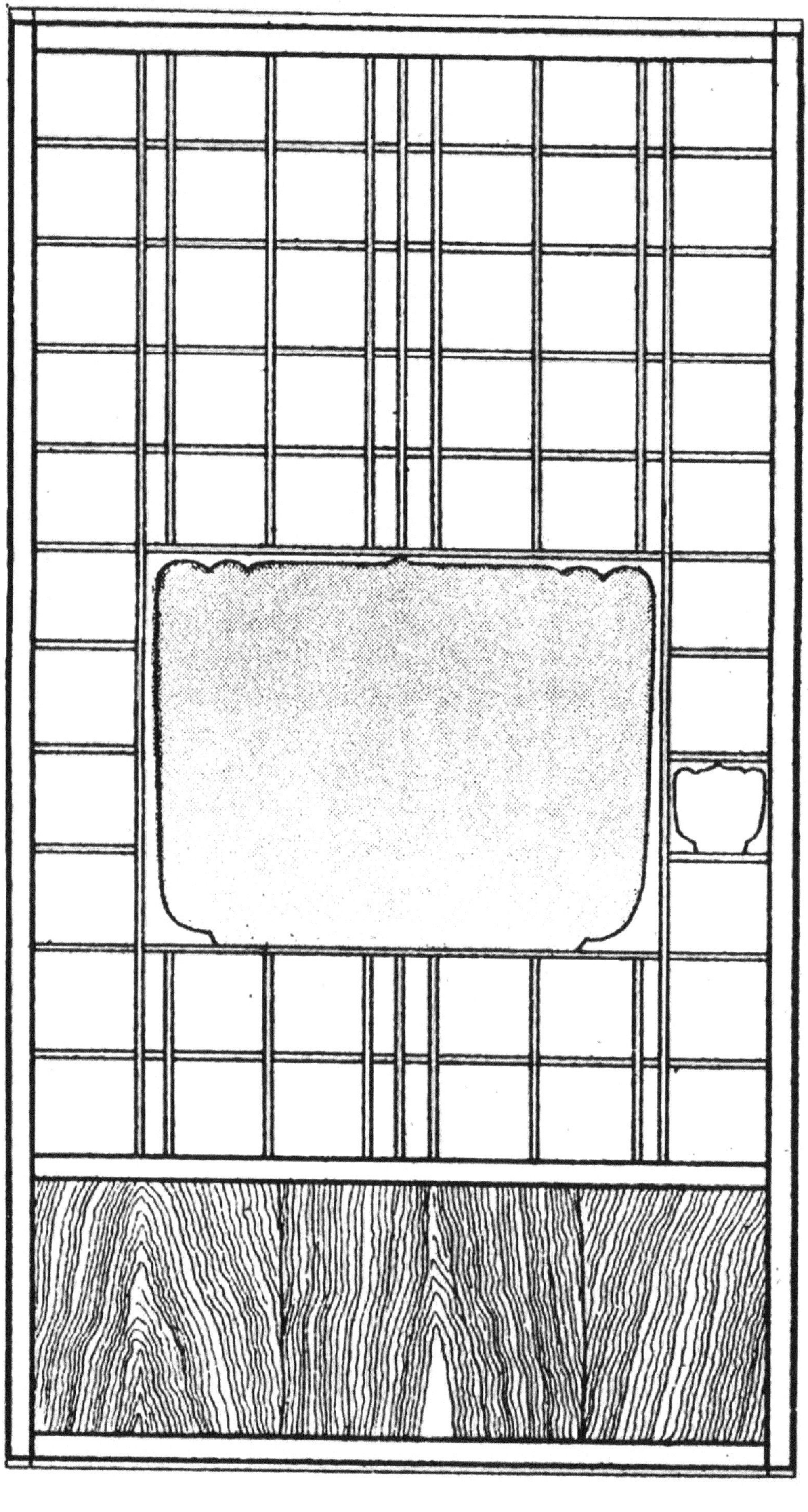

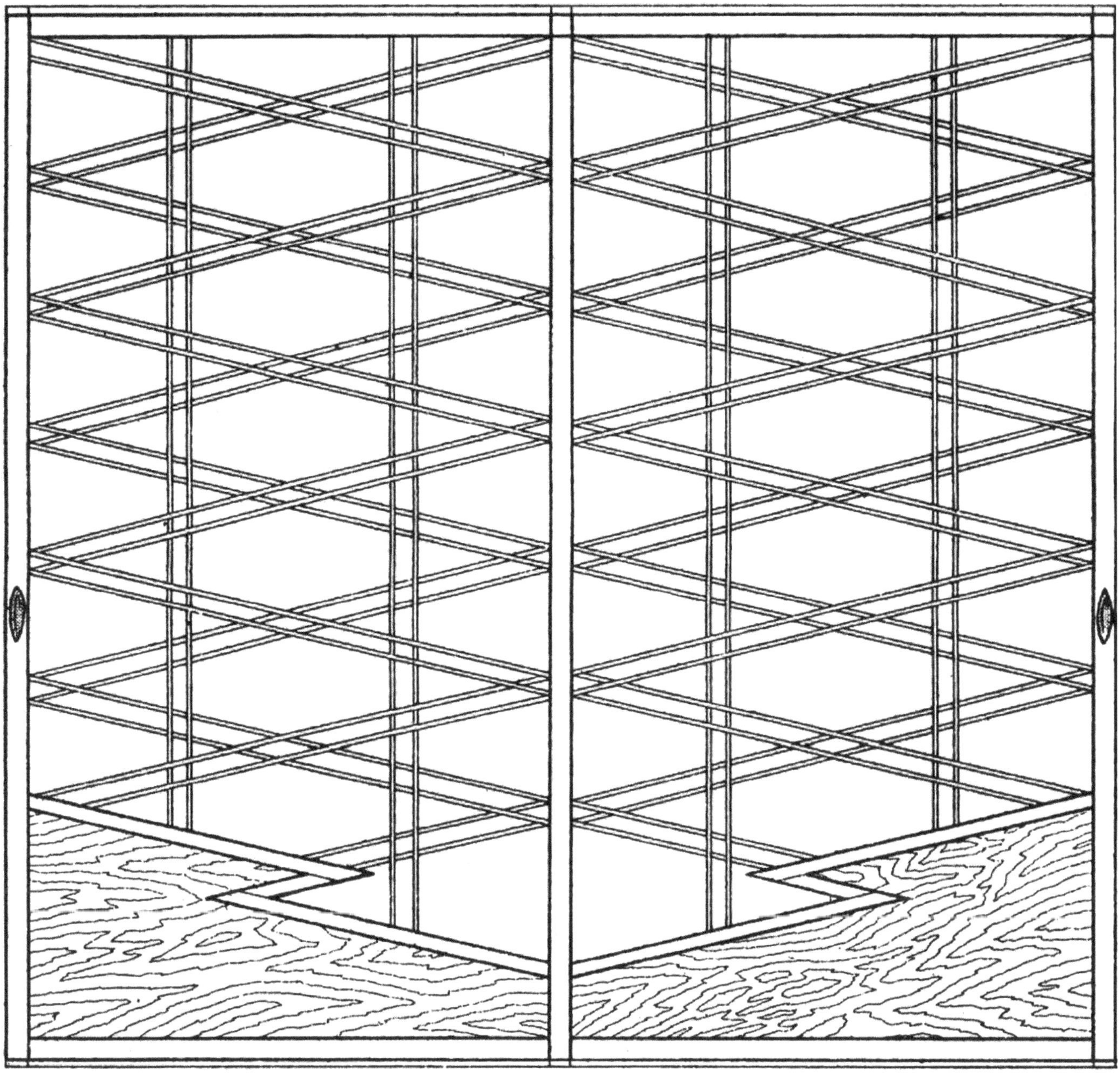

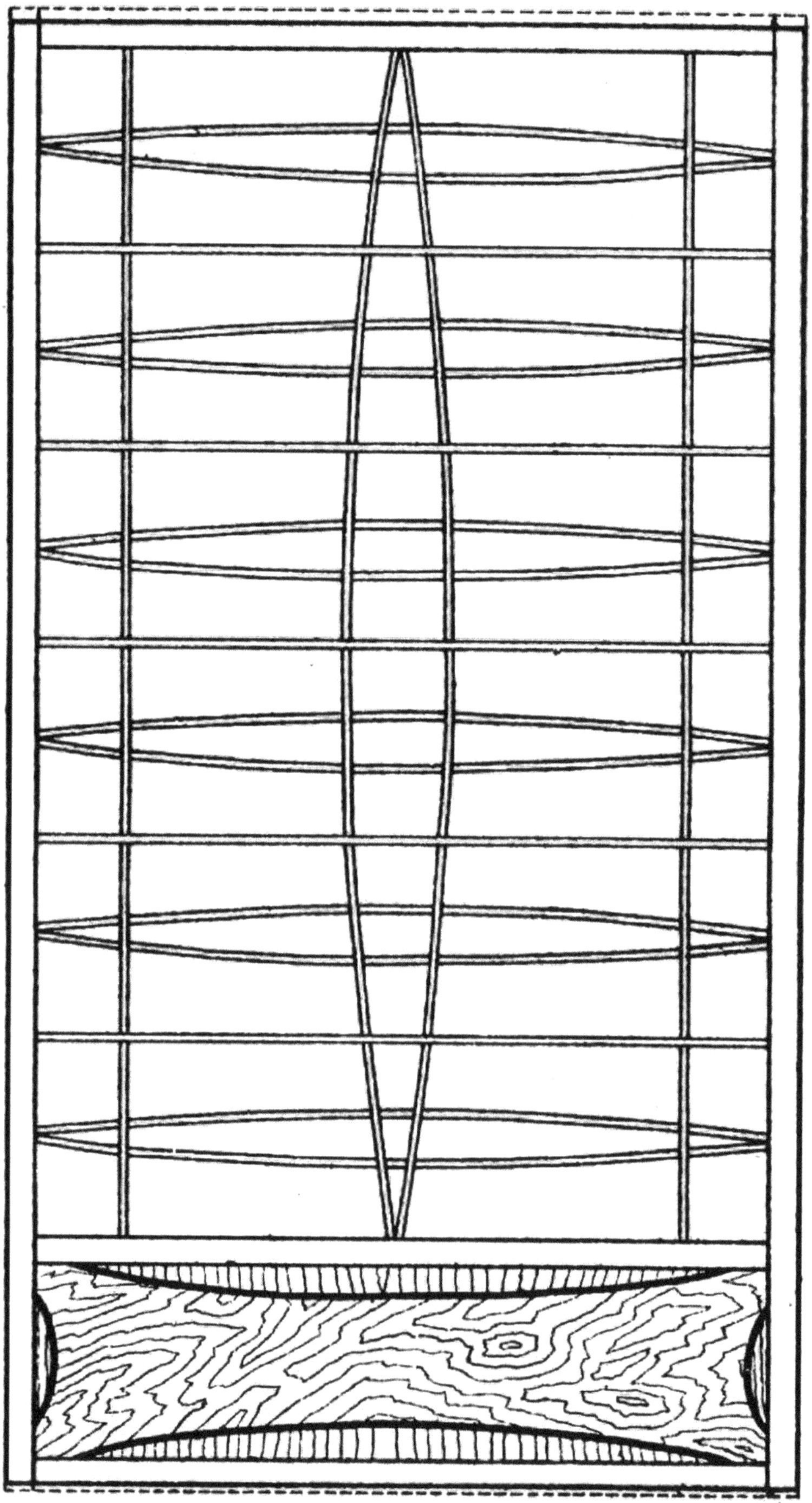

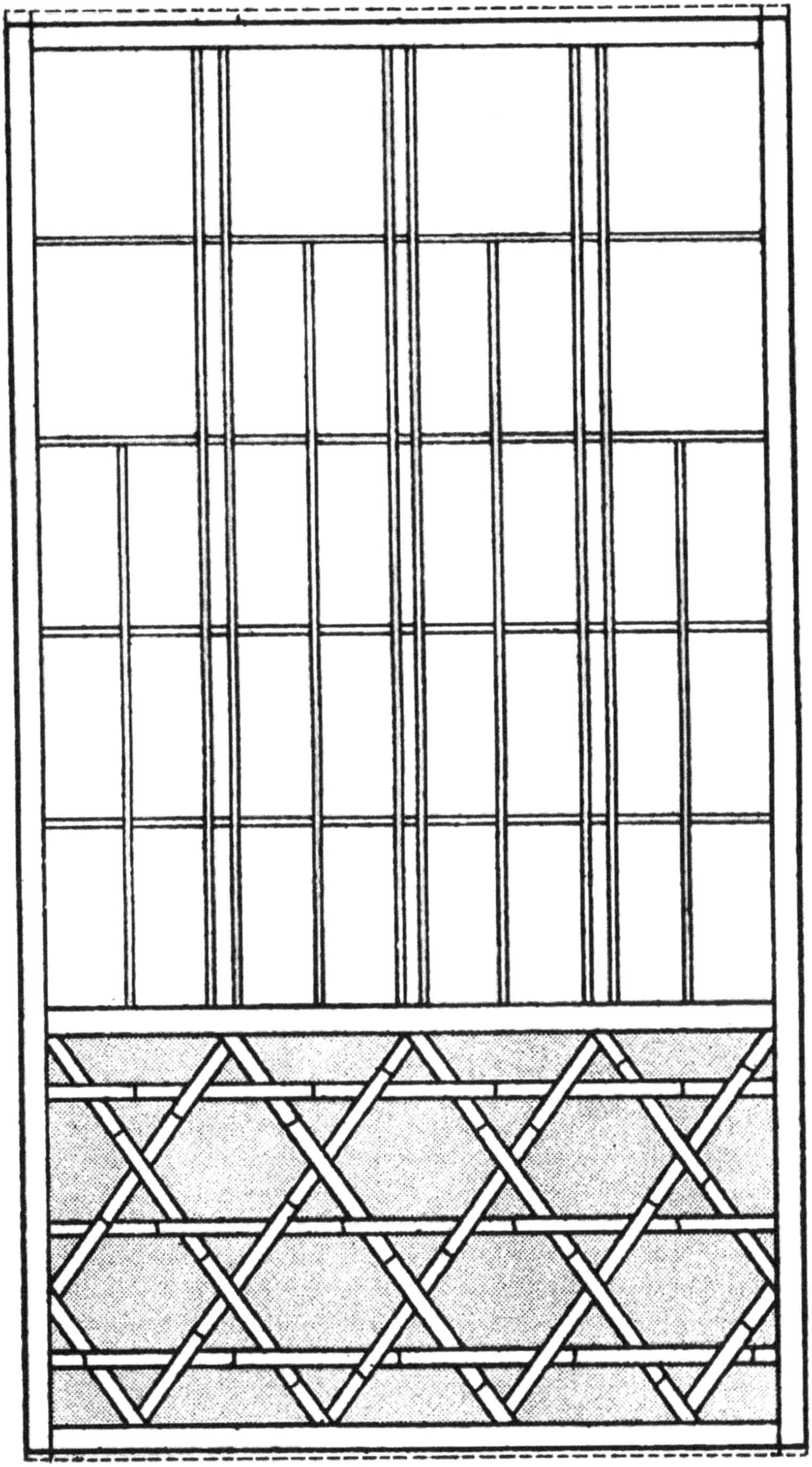

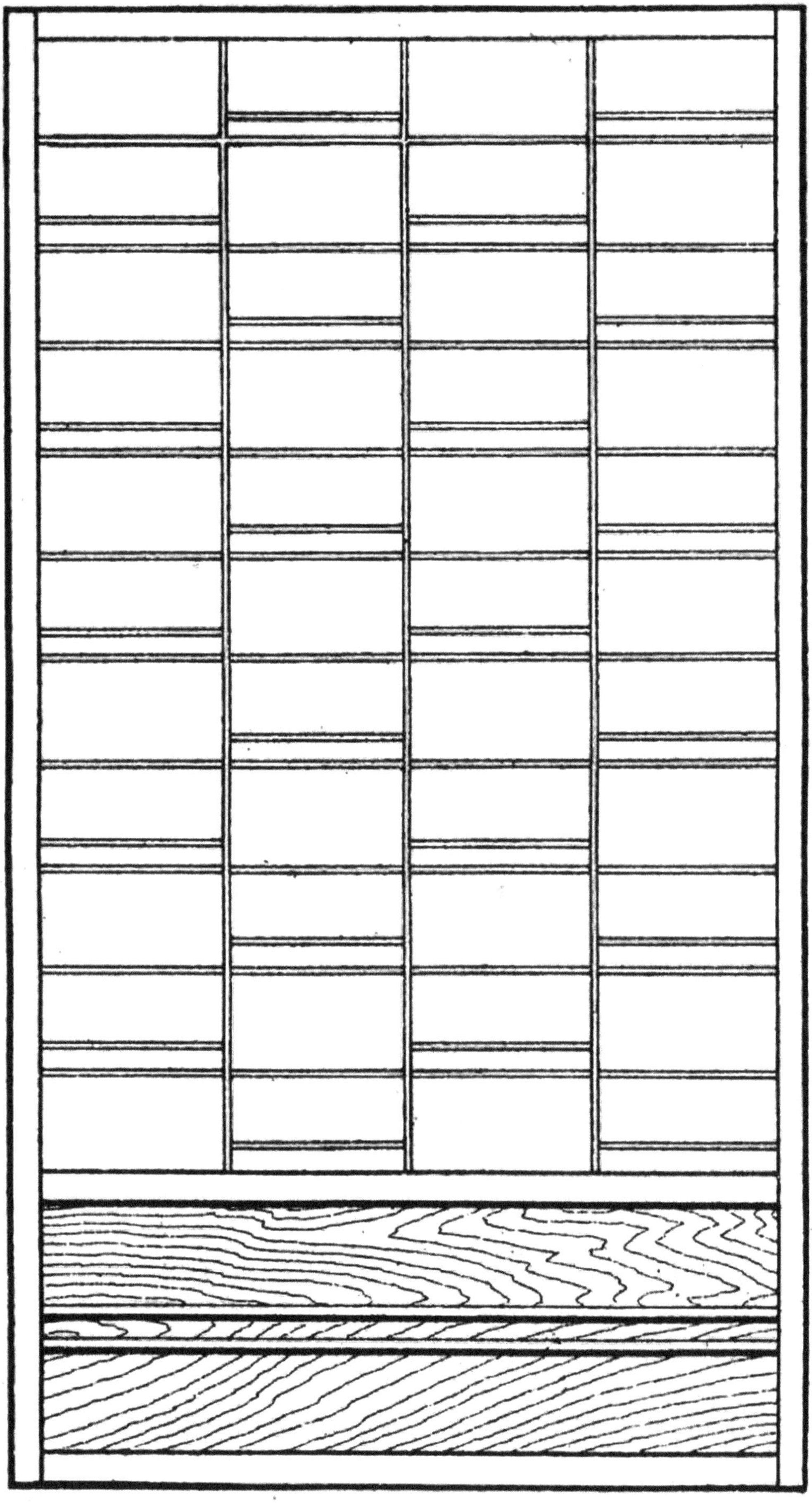

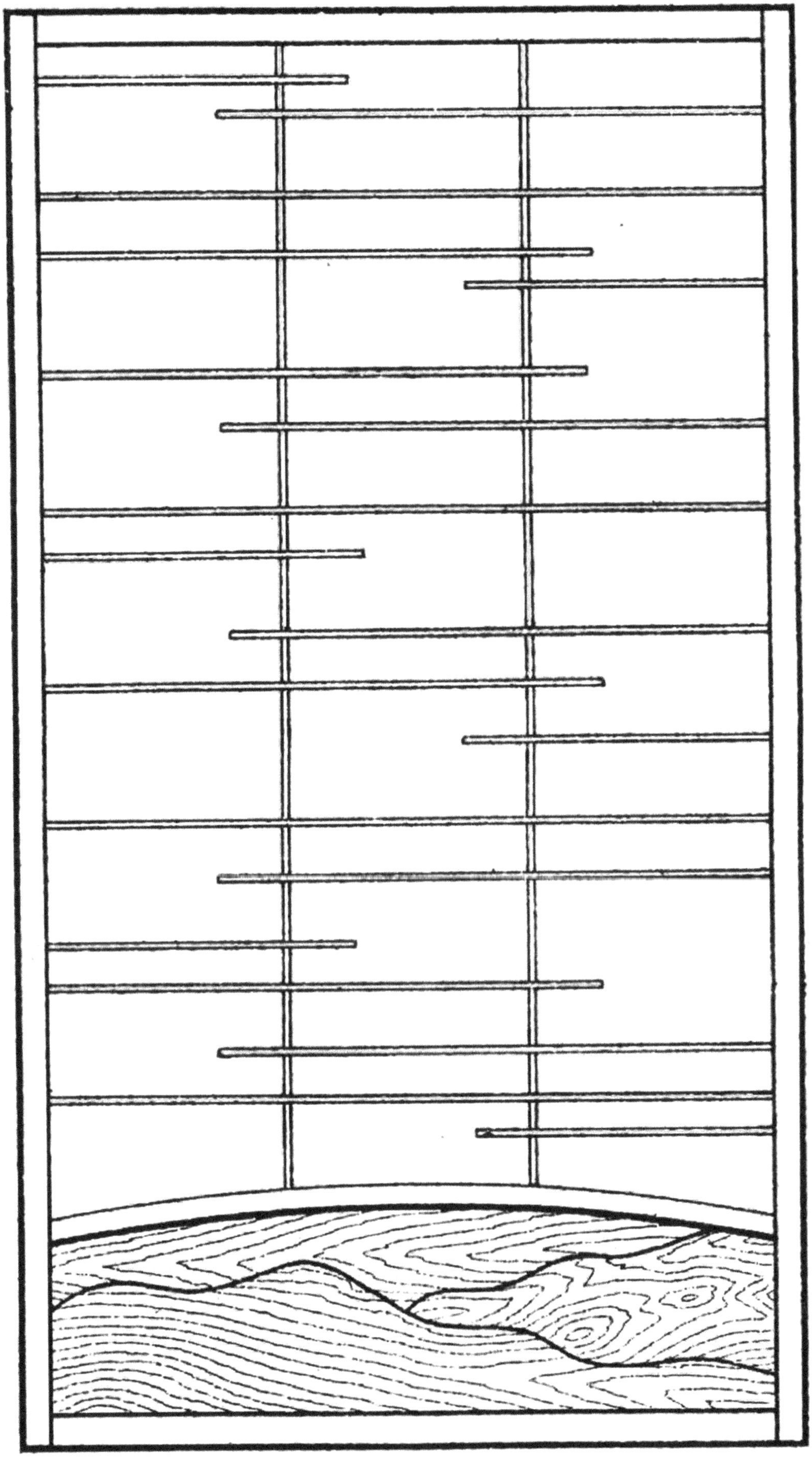

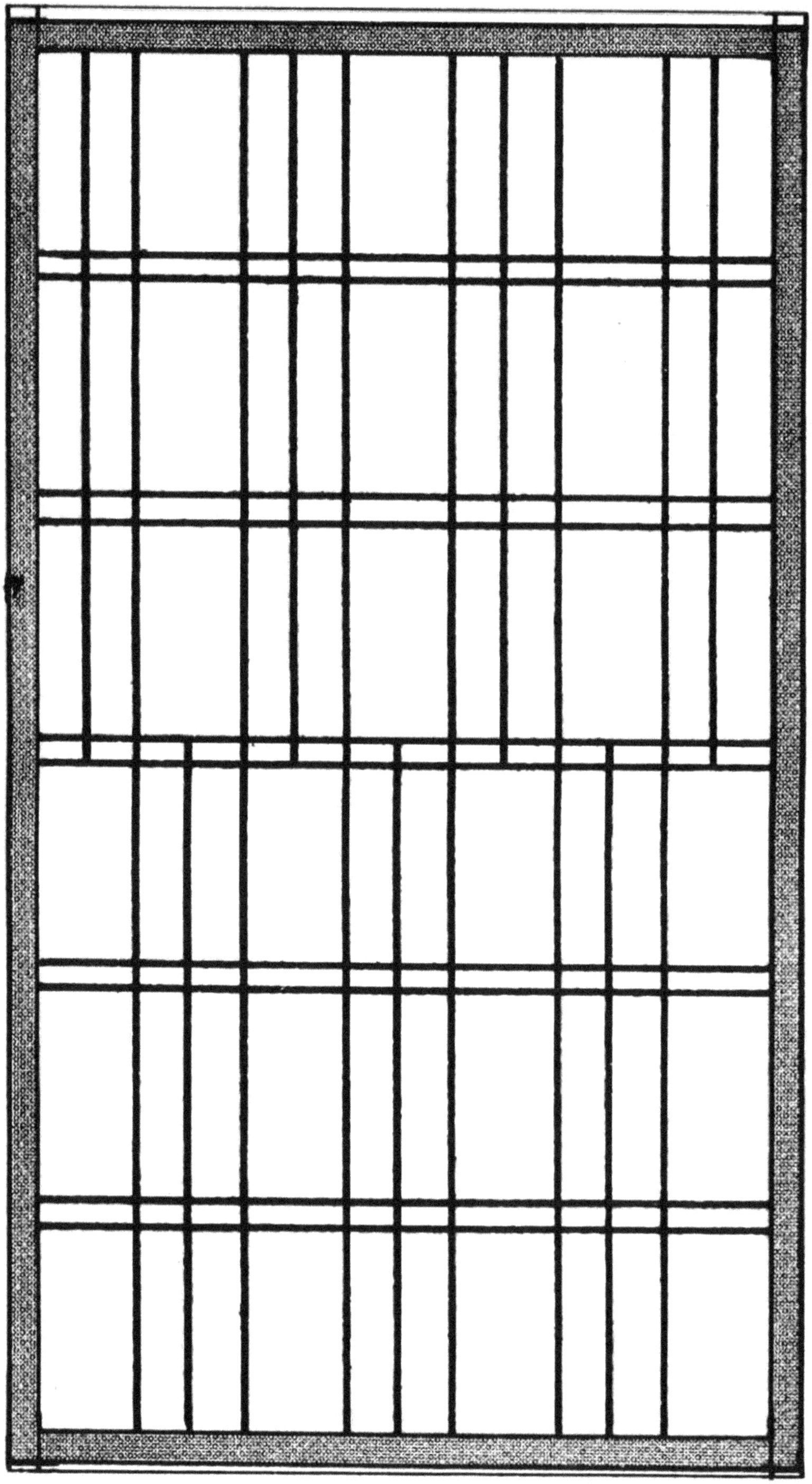

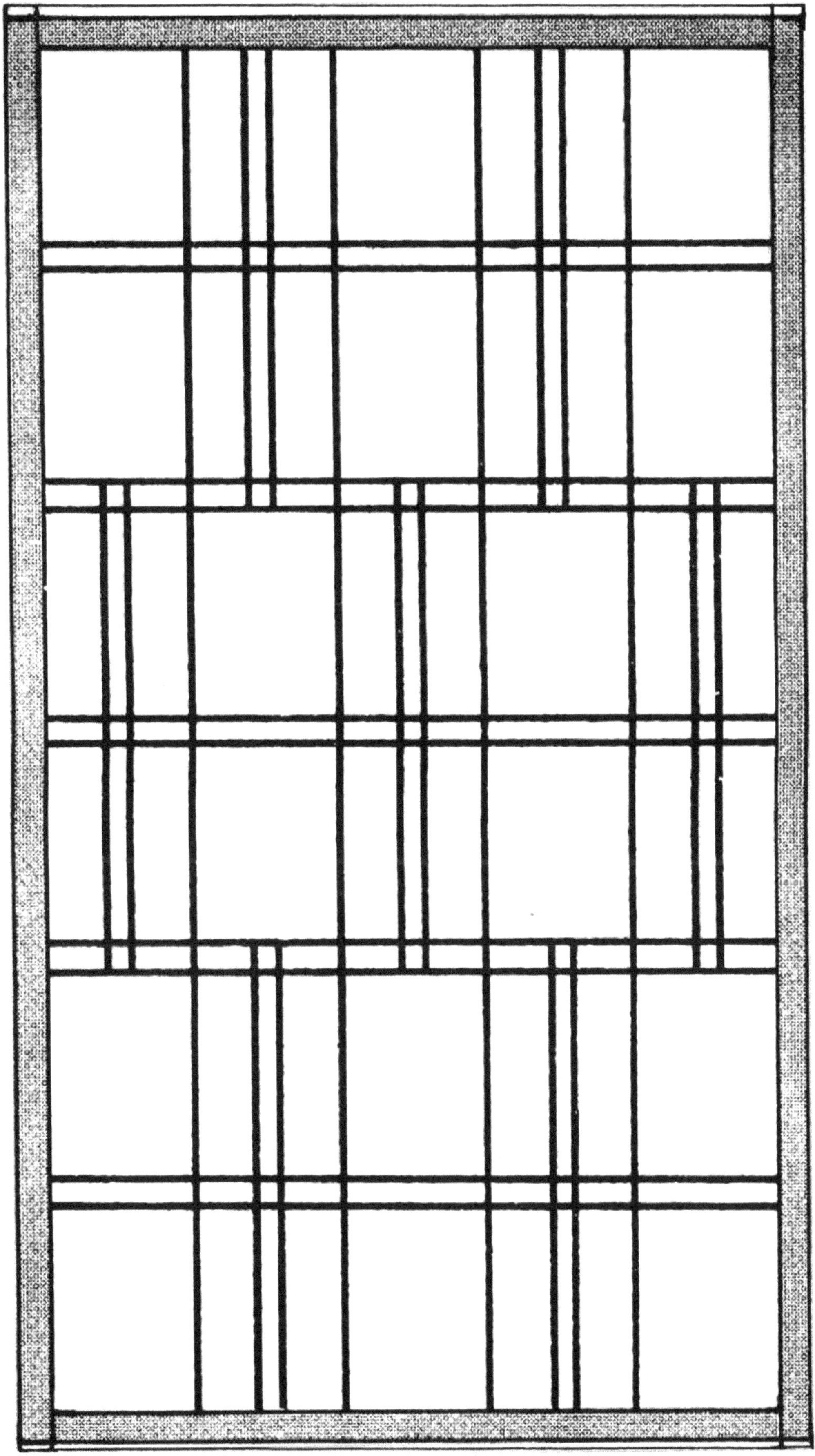

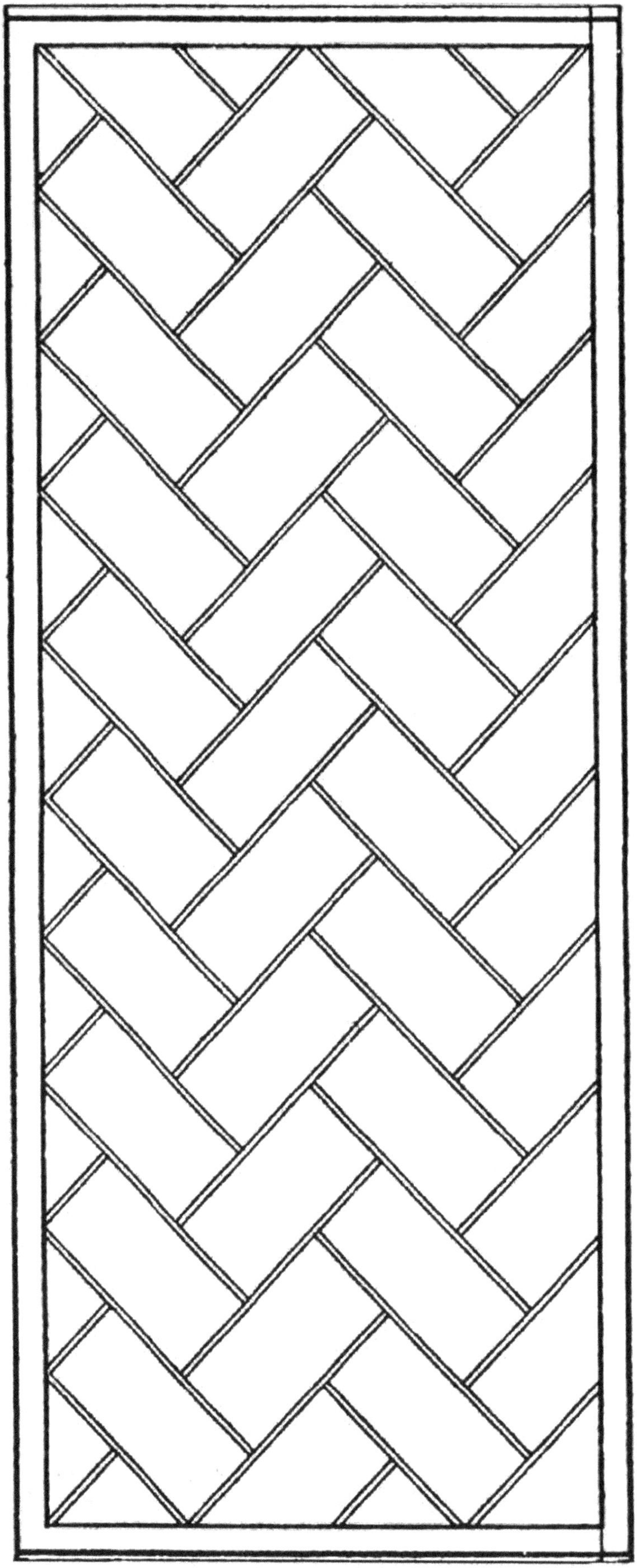

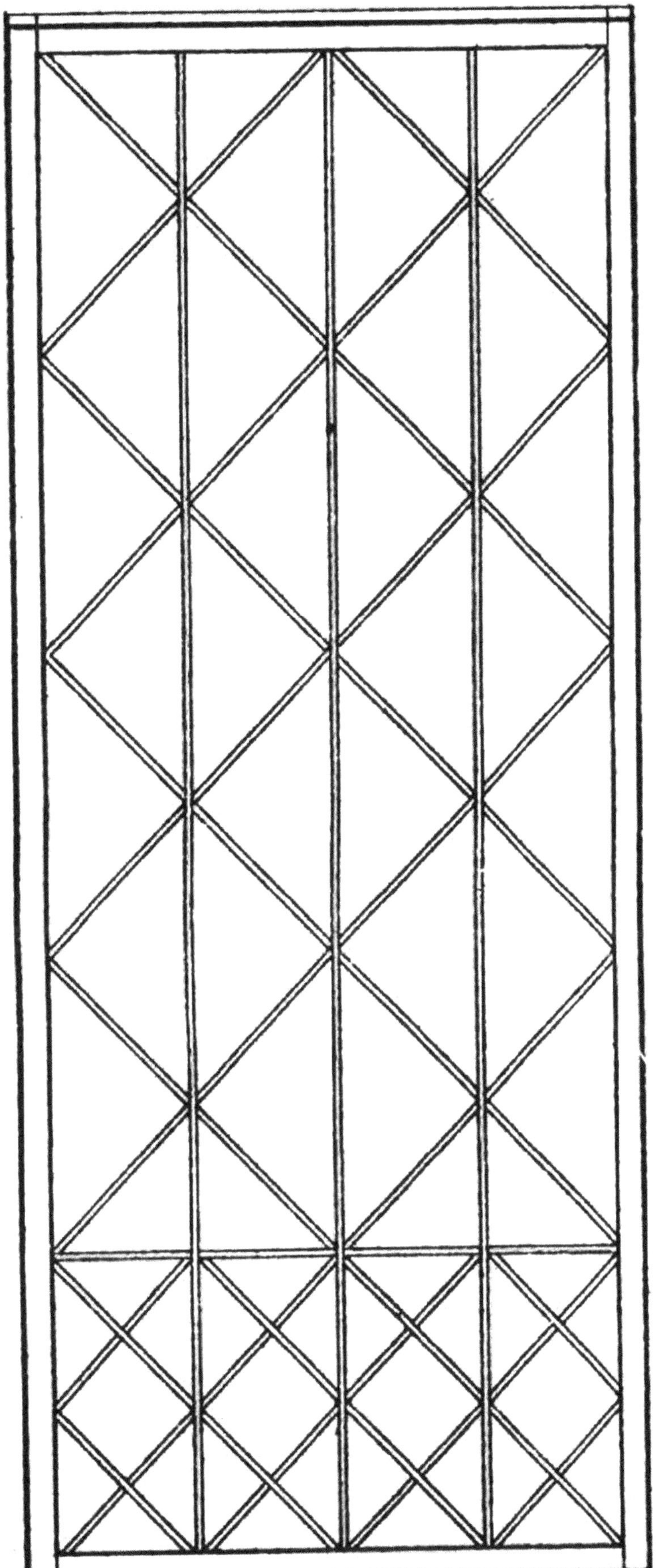

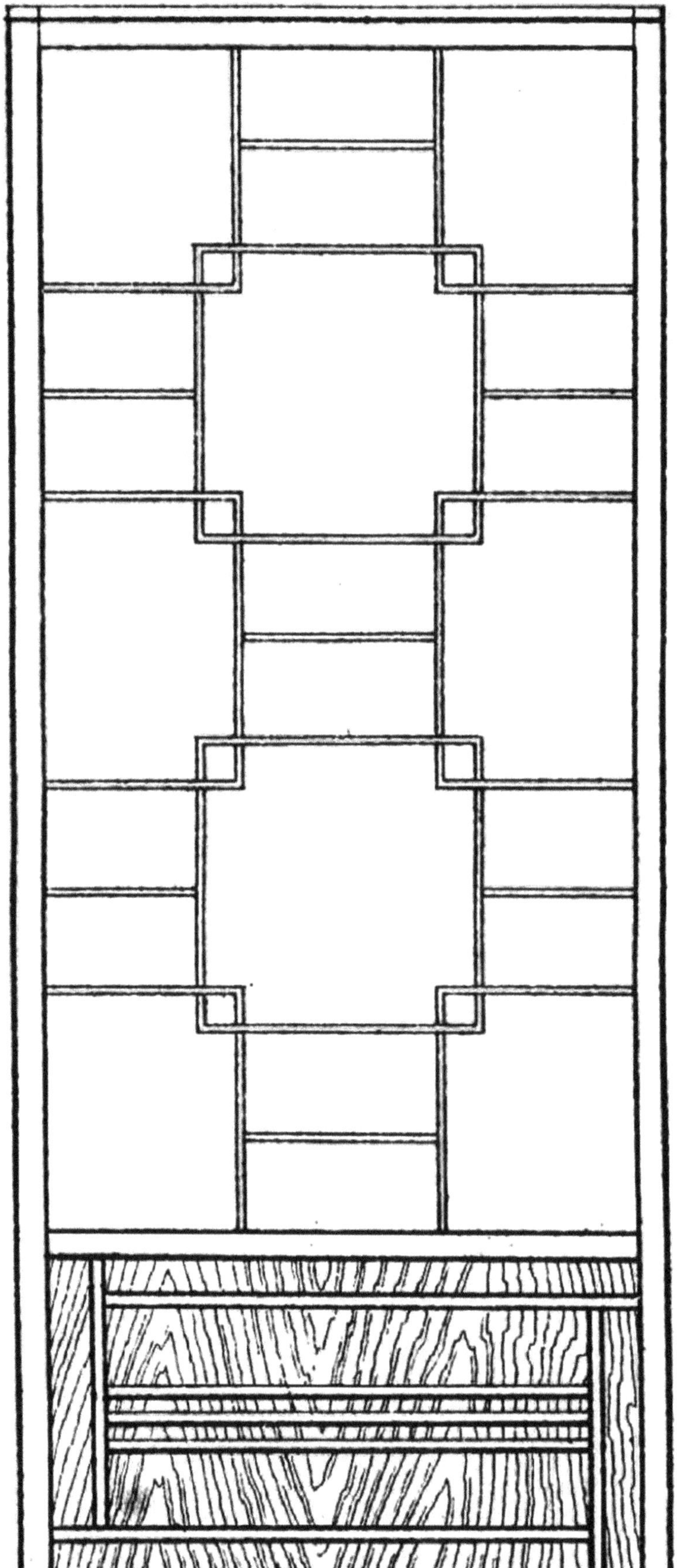

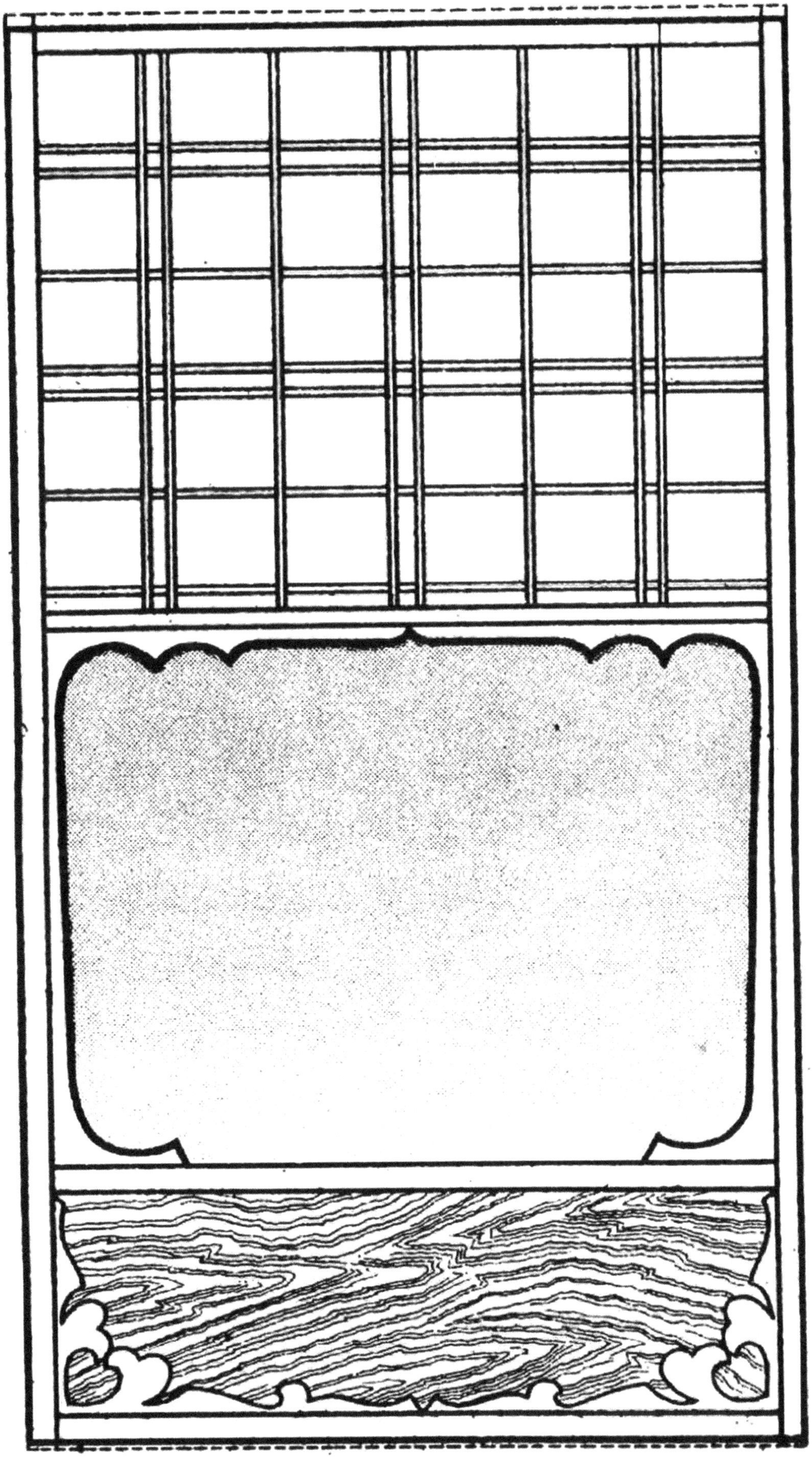

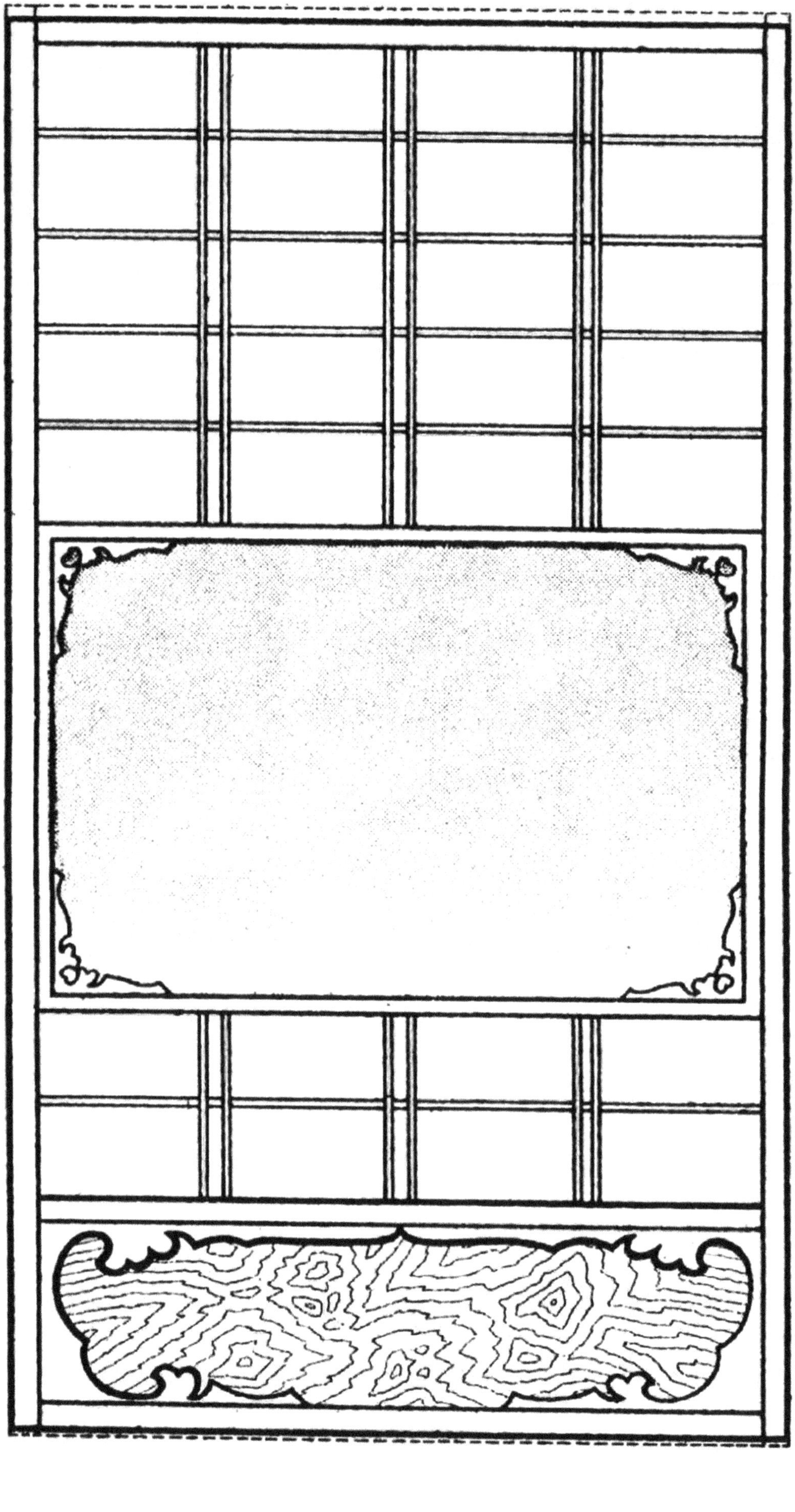

www.ingramcontent.com/pod-product-compliance
Ingram Content Group UK Ltd.
Pitfield, Milton Keynes, MK11 3LW, UK
UKHW062001290726
14090UKWH00021B/1323

9 781087 817187